SEEING IS
BELIEVING

SEEING IS BELIEVING

An Introduction to Visual Communication

Second Edition

Arthur Asa Berger

<small>SAN FRANCISCO STATE UNIVERSITY</small>

MAYFIELD PUBLISHING COMPANY

Mountain View, California
London • Toronto

Library of Congress Cataloging-in-Publication Data

Berger, Arthur Asa,
    Seeing is believing : an introduction to visual communication /
Arthur Asa Berger.
        p.   cm.
    Includes bibliographical references and index.
    ISBN 1-55934-909-3
    1. Visual communication.   I. Title.
P93.5.B445   1997
302.23—dc21   97-10862
                                                        CIP

Manufactured in the United States of America
7 8 9 0   DOC/DOC   0 9 8 7 6 5 4 3

Mayfield Publishing Company
1280 Villa Street
Mountain View, California 94041

Sponsoring editor, Holly J. Allen; production editor, Carla L. White; manuscript editor, Tom Briggs; design manager, Susan Breitbard; text designer, Anna George; cover design, Joan Greenfield; art manager, Amy Folden; manufacturing manager, Randy Hurst. The text was set in 10.5/12 Berkeley by Thompson Type and printed on 50# Finch Opaque by R. R. Donelley & Sons Company.

PREFACE

In 1989, when I published the first edition of *Seeing Is Believing,* I felt it was important to help students learn some of the most fundamental things about visual communication. That is, I wanted to help my readers develop their "visual literacy"—their ability to interpret and create visual communication. Now, in an era when visual images are playing an increasingly important role in our politics, our entertainments, and our everyday lives, I think developing visual literacy is even more crucial than ever. We must learn how to examine and to interpret images and other kinds of visual communication to determine better what impact these phenomena may be having upon our lives.

In this second edition, I have added new material on a number of topics such as communication models, ethics, postmodernism, animation, and how the eyes process visual information. I have also expanded my checklists for studying advertisements and television commercials, enhanced my discussion of semiotics, color, and MTV and added many new and interesting images.

I hope that this revised edition of *Seeing Is Believing* will help students learn how to analyze and interpret visual communication better and to understand the role it plays in their lives, the lives of their friends and families, and in society.

THE AUDIENCE

In recent years there has been a rapidly developing movement in our colleges
and universities, especially in schools of communication and journalism, to
do something about what can be described as the "visual illiteracy" of many
of our students. It is possible, and quite likely often the case, that our students graduate without knowing very much (if anything at all) about how
images communicate and people find meaning in them, about typefaces and
graphic design, or about the difference between the film image and the television image.

Ironically, a significant number of our students hope to work in fields
such as advertising, public relations, television, or journalism—fields where
they will be involved, either directly or indirectly, with visual communication. Visual communication plays an important role in everyone's lives; we
all watch television, we read newspapers and magazines and books, and we
go to the movies. And we all live in an "information" society where much of
the information we consider has a visual nature. It is important that everyone
know something about how images function and how people learn to "read"
or interpret images and various forms of visual communication. But it is
particularly important that students in communication (and related areas)
do so since those who create and use images have a responsibility to those
who will be affected by them.

MASS MEDIA FOCUS

One of the distinctive features of this book is that it focuses upon the mass
media and deals with material of interest to students, material with which
they are familiar. In this respect it differs from a number of books that deal
primarily with visual communication as it relates to the fine arts.

USE OF SEMIOLOGICAL AND PSYCHOLOGICAL CONCEPTS

Seeing Is Believing uses semiotic and psychological concepts to help readers
gain an understanding of how we find meaning in visual phenomena and
how our minds process images. These concepts are presented in a readable
manner, and numerous illustrations are offered to show how the principles
discussed have been applied. These theoretical discussions are supplemented
by a number of quotations from authorities that students will find useful
and that will help them better understand the principles of semiotics and
psychology.

SETTING A GOOD EXAMPLE

A great deal of attention was paid to the design of *Seeing Is Believing*; a book on visual communication should be attractive and show what good design is instead of merely talking about it. The book uses the power of graphic design and the visual image to facilitate learning. This book was designed by a sought-after book designer, Anna George. In addition, the images are quite remarkable and were chosen to illustrate, in a very direct and forceful manner, the topics discussed in the book.

TEACHABILITY

Seeing Is Believing was written to be a teachable book:

- It is written in an accessible style.
- It deals with topics that are of interest to students and that are part of their experience.
- It has arresting and remarkable images and visual materials to illustrate these topics.
- It is designed to be functional; that is, the book explains a number of concepts that readers can then use to interpret the images all around them. In addition, they are asked to use these concepts and ideas in interesting and creative ways.

Thus, at the end of each chapter, a section of "Applications" requires readers to think about the textual material and then apply what they have learned in doing various projects—projects that they will frequently find entertaining.

A manual for teachers is available from the publisher; it contains a number of additional activities and exercises—to be used in the classroom or as assignments—as well as discussion questions and test questions.

THE STYLE OF THE BOOK

Although the book deals with matters that are often complicated, the style of writing is, as has been suggested, readable. It might also be described as informal and perhaps even "breezy," though the latter term might be a bit extreme.

This style of writing was adopted consciously as a means of attracting the attention and maintaining the interest of the reader. The writing "sugar coats the didactic pill" as a means of enticing students to deal with material that is occasionally technical and that they might otherwise try to avoid.

In other words, this book might not strike some as reading like a textbook; it also, to my way of thinking, is so attractively designed that it doesn't look like a textbook.

There is also a good deal of humor in *Seeing Is Believing,* another means of making it more attractive and less anxiety-provoking for its intended readers. (This may be a rationalization. The author is a humorist who, like many professors, sees himself as "really" being in training to be a stand-up comedian.)

If readers find this book entertaining, half the battle will have been won. And if there are a number of ideas as well as illustrations and images (by the author and others) that amuse readers and help humanize this text and make it more attractive to its readers, so much the better. The most important thing is to get students to read the book and learn something about visual communication.

THANKS

I want to thank my editor, Holly Allen; my production editor, Carla White; my art editor, Amy Folden; and all the other people at Mayfield and elsewhere who helped me publish this second edition. I also appreciate the efforts of my copy editor, Tom Briggs; my book designer, Anna George; and all the people who were kind enough to give me permission to use their wonderful images. I'd like to thank the following people who reviewed the manuscript: Lisa L. Heinrich, St. Cloud State University; Janette Kenner Muir, George Mason University; and Wayne Wanta, University of Oregon.

CONTENTS

PHOTOGRAPHY: THE CAPTURED MOMENT   73

FILM: THE MOVING IMAGE   95

6 **TELEVISION: THE EVER-CHANGING MEDIUM   113**

7 **COMICS, CARTOONS, AND ANIMATION: THE DEVELOPMENT OF AN ART FORM   131**

IMAGE AND IMAGINATION

Images are something of a mystery to us, even though they pervade our lives. How do we make sense of them? How is it they have the power to generate emotional responses in us? These are some of the questions we must deal with when we think about images.

IMAGE

We live in a world of things seen, a world that is visual, and we expend much of our physical and emotional energy on the act of seeing. Like fish, we "swim" in a sea of images, and these images help shape our perceptions of the world and of ourselves. It is estimated, for example, that most of us receive more than 80 percent of our information through our eyes.

Images pervade our societies; we find them on billboards; in newspapers and magazines; on film screens and television screens; in our snapshots of children, friends, and relatives; in the paintings on our walls. These paint-ings, for example, both enrich our lives and convey to others something about our aesthetic sensibilities, socioeconomic class, and taste.

We communicate through images. Visual communication is a central as-pect of our lives, and much of this communication is done indirectly, through symbolic means: by words and signs and symbols of all kinds. Our emotional states and our creative impulses need some kind of visual and symbolic expression to develop and maintain themselves, which explains why many organizations pay so much attention to visual phenomena such as costumes

1

and uniforms, symbolic objects, signs, flags, and portraits and statues of important figures.

These images are needed to make philosophical abstractions or important figures from the past more real or concrete and to channel or focus our emotions more directly. It is very difficult to get emotionally involved with an abstraction, and so religious and political groups focus much attention on heroes and heroines, on great figures—who can be portrayed visually, with whom people can identify, and whose beliefs people can internalize.

In his classic *Guide to the Perplexed,* the great medieval Jewish philosopher and sage Maimonides (A.D. 1135–1204) dealt with images. He compared the concept of image (*tzelem* in Hebrew) with that of likeness (*demut* in Hebrew) and of form (*taoro* in Hebrew) in order to understand the meaning of the phrase in Genesis, "Let us make man in our image." As he wrote:

> Image (tzelem) and likeness (demut). People have thought that in the Hebrew language image denotes the shape and configuration of a thing. This supposition led them to the pure doctrine of the corporeality of God, on account of His saying, "Let us make man in our image, after our likeness" (Gen. 1:26). For they thought that God has a man's form, I mean his shape and configuration. The pure doctrine of the corporeality of God was a necessary consequence to be accepted by them.

But, as Maimonides explained a few paragraphs later (and I am greatly simplifying his argument), the statement "Let us make man in our image" refers to God's form, not his (or her) visual image, and form involves intellectual apprehension, not shape and configuration, as Maimonides defined them.

IMAGINATION

Imagination refers to the remarkable power our minds have to form a mental image of something unreal or not present and to use this power creatively—to invent new images and ideas. We can see a strong link between the terms *image* and *imagination.* Imagination exists in the mind, while the image—for our purposes—is tangible and visual. But the image is often a product of imagination, which means that the visible image is strongly connected to the mental one.

Creativity is defined in many different ways, and numerous theories try to explain what it is and why some people are creative and others are not (or don't seem to be). There seems to be a link between creativity and imagination—our ability to generate images in our minds, images *not* always representational or connected to anything in our experience.

▌ FIGURE 0.1
A rendering of a famous image—a snake with its tail in its mouth—found originally in a third-century B.C. Greek manuscript. The nineteenth-century chemist Kekule had a dream about a snake with its tail in its mouth, and this dream image led him to discover the molecular structure of benzene.

Visual images help us discover things. In *Man and His Symbols,* the psychologist Carl G. Jung recounts the role dream images played in the discovery of benzene. Jung writes (1964:26):

> The 19th-century German chemist Kekule, researching into the molecular structure of benzene, dreamed of a snake with its tail in its mouth. [A representation of this from a third-century B.C. Greek manuscript is shown in Figure 0.1.] He interpreted the dream to mean that the structure was a closed carbon ring . . . [Figure 0.2].

▌ FIGURE 0.2
A rendering of the closed carbon ring that Kekule drew in his *Textbook of Organic Chemistry* (1861).

This anecdote suggests that there is a strong link between visual images and what we call creativity. The images we see, whether in our dreams or daydreams, in drawings and doodles in our notebooks, or images we find in printed matter or films or the broadcast media—all are connected to our ability to focus our attention on something, to deal with it in other than abstract and intellectual ways, and ultimately to "break set" (escape from conventional ideas and beliefs) and come up with something new. If necessity is the mother of invention, the visual image is its father.

THE VISUAL AND THE PSYCHE

Images have the power to reveal our mental states. The neurologist and founder of psychoanalysis Sigmund Freud, in an early formulation, described the *psyche* as being divided into two parts: one accessible to our consciousness and one buried beneath our consciousness, an "unconscious." (There is actually a third part of the psyche, the preconscious, just below consciousness, which is accessible to our consciousness.) We can represent the psyche by an iceberg. The conscious element is the small part of the iceberg that is above the waves. Just underneath the waves, there is an area we can see into, which is the preconscious. Underneath the preconscious is a huge mass, which we cannot see and which is not accessible to consciousness, that represents the unconscious.

Freud also explained, in a later refinement on his theories, that the psyche comprises three elements: the *id,* the *ego,* and the *superego.* The id represents drives, impulses, and sexual desire. The superego embodies moral beliefs (conscience) and ideal aspirations. The ego mediates between the two forces and involves the way individuals relate to their environment. The ego employs various defense mechanisms to achieve a balance between the forces of the id and superego. One of the most important of these defense mechanisms is sublimation, which involves the redirection of id energy from sexual matters to other areas, such as artistic expression. (Freud's theory is one explanation of artistic creativity.)

Jung, another great psychologist, had a different set of concepts. He believed there were archetypes, "universal images" that were found in myths, dreams, religions, and works of art. These archetypes were reflections of what Jung called the "collective unconscious," a concept that is extremely controversial. (We can see how a person has an unconscious, but it is difficult to explain the existence of a *collective* unconscious.) The hero, according to Jungians, is the most important archetype.

The psyche, according to Jung, is divided into the shadow (the dark side that is kept hidden from consciousness) and the ego (the light side). But the shadow contains some positive elements, such as creativity, and the ego contains some negative elements, such as destructive attitudes. Jungians also believe that men have a feminine side, the anima, and women have a masculine side, the animus, which play an important role in human development. In sum, Jungians offer a considerably different understanding of the human psyche and of dreams and images than Freudians do, though both believe in the importance of the unconscious.

In 1977, a German therapist, Anneliese Ude-Pestel, wrote *Betty: History and Art of a Child in Therapy,* a book about one of her patients—a little girl who was significantly disturbed (if not almost psychotic). Betty loved to make drawings and had done hundreds of them, which her father had saved. The paintings were all ghastly—full of monsters and horrifying images, reflecting her psychological state. As the treatment progressed, Betty's drawings changed—and by the end of the therapy, when Betty had been restored to mental health, her drawings were those of a typical little girl (Figures 0.3, 0.4, and 0.5).

The visual image, we see, has the capacity to show the anguish of a tormented soul just as it has the power to stimulate sexual desire, to generate intense feelings, to lead people to perform selfless acts of bravery or cruel acts of barbarism. It is not the image or symbol itself that is responsible, but rather the ability of the image to evoke responses in people that are connected to their beliefs and values.

▌ **Figure 0.3**
Betty's drawing, *Strangled Deadman*, drawn when she was six years old, before she started therapy.

▌ **Figure 0.4**
Indian Girl on the Cross, drawn by Betty in the middle of her therapy.

▌ **Figure 0.5**
Dancing Girl, by Betty. This picture was drawn by Betty near the end of her therapy and reflects her progress in overcoming her problems and becoming a normal little girl.

This power means, of course, that those who create images and symbols must think about the moral implications of what they do. Those individuals who, in some almost magical way (which they may not completely understand themselves), have the ability to harness the power of the image must take responsiblity for what they do. To the extent that seeing is believing, we must make sure that the images we create do not generate beliefs that are individually or socially destructive.

THE FUNCTIONS OF ART

In his book *The Unchanging Arts: New Forms for the Traditional Functions of Art in Society,* the art historian Alan Gowans suggests that the arts have always performed one (or more) of the functions on the following page.

1. Substitute imagery
2. Illustration
3. Persuasion/conviction
4. Beautification

Gowans (1971:12, 13) explains his theory as follows:

> Instead of asking "What is Art?" we need to ask "What kinds of things have been done by that activity traditionally called Art?" And then we will find that activity historically performed four functions: substitute imagery; illustration; conviction and persuasion; and beautification. (1) In cases where the appearance of something needed to be preserved for one reason or another, art made pictures that could be substituted for the actual thing. (2) Art made images or shapes (including pictographs) that could be used in whole or part to tell stories or record events vividly ("illustrate," "illuminate," "elucidate" all come from the same root "lux" = "light"). (3) Art made images which by association of shapes with ideas set forth the fundamental convictions or realized ideals of societies (usually in more ephemeral media). (4) Art beautified the world by pleasing the eye or gratifying the mind; what particular combination of forms, arrangements, colors, proportions or ornament accomplished this end in any given society depended, of course, on what kinds of illustration or conviction or persuasion a given society required its arts to provide.

Whenever we look at any work of art or any image (or visual field in general), we might consider what the "function" of the work is—as far as the viewer, the creator, society in general, and anyone else is concerned—and which of these four functions is dominant. We might also think about how an image is affected by the medium in which it is found and how a given work relates to other works. (Many works consciously or unconsciously borrow from other works—a phenomenon known as *intertextuality*.)

AN EXPERIMENT

In the pages that follow, you will find a number of images to examine (Figures 0.6–0.15). Instead of glancing at these images for the two or three seconds we ordinarily devote to such things (when flipping through a magazine, for instance), please study these works carefully. Then answer the following questions:

1. *What kinds of feelings did each of the works generate in you?* If you felt nothing, why not? If you felt strong emotions, how do you explain this? Did you, for example, experience envy, desire, anxiety, fear, repulsion, sadness, or joy? If so, why?

2. *To which element in your psyche* (id, ego, superego) *did each of the works primarily relate?* Why?

3. *Which of the four functions of art* (as explained by Alan Gowans) *dominated each image or work?* If you had trouble deciding the answer to this question, how do you explain that? Are there other functions that Gowans missed? If so, what are they?

4. *If you were asked to select some of these works to appear at the beginning of a book on visual communication, which ones would you choose?* How would you explain your choice of each work?

5. *Do you find any unifying element in the works selected?* If so, what is it?

6. *If you were asked to make an exhibition of a number of works of art, images, or visual phenomena that expressed your personality, what would you choose?*

7. *If you had to choose ten images to represent America, which images would you choose?*

8. *When was the last time you made a drawing or painting?* If you have not done one for a long time, how come? Why is it that when we are young children we love to draw, but when we get older we generally give it up?

▌ **FIGURE 0.6**
Ridley Scott, "1984"
Macintosh commercial still,
taken from television
screen.

▌ Figure 0.7
This self-portrait by Richard Shaw looks like a painting, but it is actually a photograph. Why does it look like a painting? How did Shaw achieve his effects?

■ **Figure 0.8**
"1984" by Thomas Porter, based on research by Robert Cook. This is a computer simulation of moving billiard balls.

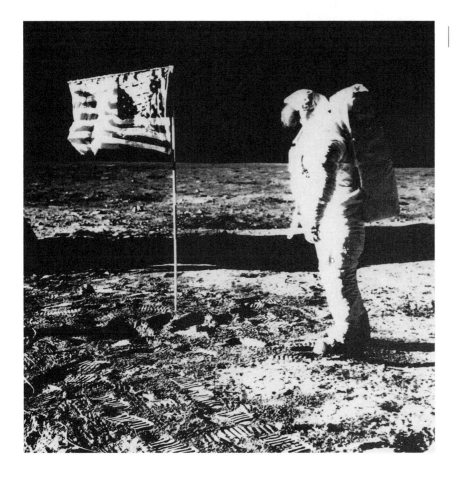

■ **Figure 0.9**
Astronaut on the moon.

FIGURE 0.10
(a) Jason Berger, *Sketch of View from Graca*, 1978.
(b) Jason Berger, *View from Graca*, 1978. Oil on canvas.

(a)

(b)

FIGURE 0.11
David Levine, *Lyndon Baines Johnson,* 1964.

FIGURE 0.12
Joan Miró, *Woman and Little Girl in Front of the Sun.* 1946. Where is the woman? Where is the little girl? Where is the sun? Does this painting strike you as whimsical and amusing or foolish?

❚ **Figure 0.14**
This image from *Rain* uses overhead shots of umbrellas to frame the figures in an artfully designed composition. The overhead shot, its simplicity, and its lighting—which highlights the structure of the umbrellas—all help give the image its elegance and power.

❚ **Figure 0.13**
"Mona Lisa" in Varitype.

Here are some interesting icons for you to examine. Would you say that functionality is the most important aspect of icons, or are design and aesthetic factors important as well?

 entrance   exit   information   coffee shop   taxi

 restaurant   automat   toilet   ladies' room   parking

 mens' room   baggage depot   baggage dispatch   lockers   flowers

 waiting room lost and found hairdresser bicycle dispatch general baggage

men with weapons	riders	other human figures	deer	other animals

 Numbers   AppleTalk   Monitors & Sound   Views

 Speech   Map   Users & Groups   Labels

 Color   Desktop Patterns   ~ATM™   PC Exchange

 Date & Time   Energy Saver   Mouse   WindowShade

 Startup Disk   Memory   Control Strip   TCP/IP

SEEING IS BELIEVING

Seeing is a complicated phenomenon. When we see an image, our brain breaks the image down into various components and processes them separately, before reconstituting these parts as an image. For example, the brain processes properties such as colors, textures, the edges of objects, light and shadow, and motion separately and then brings them together into an image (*how* it does this still is something of a mystery).

SEEING

The actual act of seeing is determined by the physical structure of the eye. What we perceive, of course, is affected by other factors. In *The Hidden Dimension*, Edward T. Hall describes the physical structure of the eye. He explains that the retina (the part of the eye that is sensitive to light) is composed of three main parts or areas: the fovea, the macula, and the section of the eye where peripheral vision occurs. Each of these areas performs different visual functions, enabling people to see in three somewhat different ways. Because the three types of vision occur at the same time and blend into one another, normally they aren't differentiated.

The eye, then, is an incredibly complex organ, and the mechanism of seeing, though effortless for most people, involves extremely complicated relationships between our eyes and our brains—a subject that will be discussed in a later chapter.

When we see, we are doing many things at once. We are seeing an enormous field peripherally. We are seeing in an up-to-down, left-to-right movement. We are imposing on what we are isolating in our field of vision not only implied axes to adjust balance but also a structural map to chart and measure the action of the compositional forces that are so vital to content and, therefore, to message input and output. All of this is happening while at the same time we are decoding all manner of symbols.

–DONIS A. DONDIS,
*A PRIMER OF
VISUAL LITERACY*

15

The very structure of the eye, Hall points out, has an effect on the way we design and use space. As he notes, in Western countries, we tend to focus our attention on objects, not on the spaces that separate them. By contrast, in Japan, for example (1971:75), "spaces are perceived, named, and revered as the ma, or intervening interval." We all have the same eyes, but what we see, or perhaps what we focus our attention on, differs from culture to culture.

Rudolf Arnheim suggests in *Visual Thinking* (1969:37) that

> visual perception is not a passive recording of stimulus material but an active concern of the mind. The sense of sight operates selectively. The perception of shape consists in the application of form categories, which can be called visual concepts because of their simplicity and generality. Perception involves problem solving.

The same point is made by E. H. Gombrich in *Art and Illusion* (1960:172), where he argues that perception "is always an active process, conditioned by our expectations and adapted to situations. Instead of talking about seeing and knowing, we might do a little better to talk about seeing and noticing. We notice only when we look for something." Perception is not automatic, then. It may be a bit of an exaggeration, but in many cases, we have to look for something in order to see it.

BELIEVING

What we believe depends on a number of factors, including our age, education, socioeconomic status, country, family background, and personality. Generally, when we talk about believing, it means we think that something is true. Philosophers talk about the correspondence theory of truth—the notion that there is a correspondence between what we believe and what is true about the "real world."

Our belief that things exist in the real world often is tied to what we have seen; our belief in the truth about propositions usually is tied to reasoning and inference. The title of this book, *Seeing Is Believing,* reflects people's sense, first, that if they see something, they can be confident it exists, and second, that seeing enables them to ascertain, with "their own eyes," the truth about events.

However, as this book will show, seeing isn't always a good guide to knowing what is happening. Seeing may give us a certain amount of truth, but it may not reveal the whole truth, especially because much of what we see is mediated—determined by someone else. And new computer technology enables artists, filmmakers, and the like to generate all kinds of remarkable images. We can now modify photographs, create special effects, integrate scenes from old films, incorporate dead actors and actresses into commercials, and do many other things that force us to question the relationship between seeing and believing. Much of what we see—in the media, that is—we can no longer believe.

THE SOCIAL ASPECTS OF THE VISUAL

Research suggests that many people are "obsessed" with their looks—with their hair, their faces, their complexions, their bodies, their arms and legs; and huge industries exist to help people lose weight, conquer acne, get rid of "saddles" on their hips or droopy eyelids—you name it. Surveys indicate that though people claim they choose their mates on the basis of personality, religion, occupation, and other traits, in fact, they are initially attracted to them on the basis of looks.

We gain a great deal of information about others (and provide a great deal of information about ourselves) on the basis of visual perceptions. For example, think how important our cars are to us and how important styling is for people when it comes to choosing a car. For most of us, cars are not simply a means of transportation; they are also, perhaps more importantly, statements about ourselves, our status, and our taste or style (Figure 1.1).

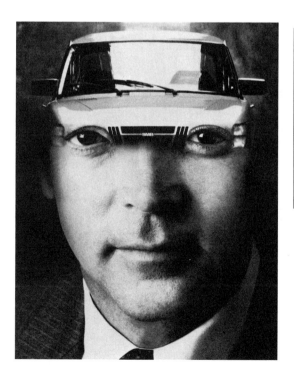

▌ FIGURE 1.1
An extremely controversial Saab advertisement. The fusion of a face and a car creates a remarkably compelling image. In making this image, it was necessary to widen the distance between the eyes of the man so that they would appear in place of the headlights, giving him a curious (and, some suggest, idiotic) look.

The same applies to our houses. People often judge us on the basis of where we live, how big our house is, what our house looks like, and whether we have a view. The way a house is decorated—the color of the walls, the kind of furniture, the spatiality—all of these things might seem trivial and insignificant, but we know that they are connected to powerful and very deep aspects of our psyches.

People also evaluate us, perhaps unconsciously, on the basis of how attractive we are and how attractive our mates are. Numerous surveys demonstrate that people judged "attractive" are generally better liked and higher rated on surveys than are people judged "unattractive." We learn whether we are attractive by the responses of others. Our identities, then, are to a great degree fashioned by what have been called "significant others" via the feedback they give us about ourselves.

This fact helps explain the anxiety people feel about "blind" dates. The term is important, for it directs our attention to the importance of the visual in our scheme of things. We might even have talked on the telephone to a so-called blind date, but because we have not seen this person, we generally feel uneasy. Numerous models and famous actresses tell tales of not having dates in high school or of having their mothers arrange for someone to take them to the prom. The same applies for many famous men—statesmen, actors, and businessmen who were not exactly social lions when young. Not having a date on a given day means absolutely nothing.

THE VISUAL AND PERSONAL IDENTITY

We've already suggested that visual perceptions confer status on people—that others evaluate us on the basis of our cars and clothes and houses and mates. The calculations these other people make generate ideas in their heads about who and what we are—about our identities.

And people often refer to us in terms of our physical attributes. Blondes supposedly "have more fun," and redheads are supposed to have tempers. Think also about baldness and the trauma it causes in men who often adopt bizarre hairstyles in a futile attempt to hide their baldness. People are also described in terms of whether they are short or tall, thin or fat (or skinny or husky), light or dark, and so on. Consider the role skin color has played in our history and in the history of many other nations.

Our physiques and other visible aspects can lead to nicknames that, it is likely, often play an important part in the way we develop our personalities. Undesirable identities probably lead to various kinds of compensating behaviors so that, to a certain degree, it might be argued that what we are or become is affected to a considerable extent by what we look like.

SEEING ISN'T BELIEVING

If visual matters are so important, it makes sense for us to understand how visual communication works—the rules, principles, and codes that people use to interpret (or misinterpret) visual phenomena. *The principles discussed in this book can be applied anywhere—in magazine design, in newspaper layout, in advertising, in photography, in film and television making, or in something as humble as writing a resume—because these principles apply wherever visual matters are important, and they are important everywhere.*

We know, from watching magicians, that we can be misled by a visual phenomenon. Magicians don't saw people in half; they only seem to. We also know that people often have delusions, see "apparitions" that really aren't there, have dreams that are "unreal," and can be fooled or misled by visual phenomena (Figures 1.2 and 1.3).

This book will help you learn how to interpret and understand visual phenomena more correctly and use them in a more reasoned manner. It will deal with principles of design and other matters involved in visual commu-

▌ FIGURE 1.2
Optical illusion, "Devil's Tuning Fork." Why is it so difficult to look at this image? That is, how does this optical illusion work?

The word "Levi's" is a registered trademark of Levi Strauss & Co., San Francisco

LEVI'S AND LEVI'S FOR GALS. PANTS MADE TO A DIFFERENT VISION.

▌ FIGURE 1.3
Levi's advertisement based on the "Devil's Tuning Fork" optical illusion.

nication; with photography, film, television, typography, comics, and cartoons; and with the relationship that exists between visual matters and the imagination.

COGNITION AND VISUAL IMAGES

We actually expend a great deal of energy in the process of seeing things. In *Understanding Video,* Jarice Hanson (1987:39) cites some fascinating statistics on this matter:

> It is estimated that 75 percent of the information entering the brain is from the eyes, and that 38 percent of the fibers entering or leaving the central nervous system are in the optic nerve. Current research indicates that the eyes have 100 million sensors in the retina, but only five million channels to the brain from the retina. This means that more information processing is actually done in the eye than in the brain, and even the eye filters out information . . .

Thus, we allocate much of our energy to processing visual information. We do this in the service of our cognitive faculties, or the means by which we acquire knowledge. This is generally done through either perception, intuition, or reasoning. For our purposes, the term *perception* will be used to deal with visual phenomena. We might, then, distinguish between *sight,* or the ability to see; *seeing,* or the actual process of using sight; and *perception,* or the ability to apprehend and know the world by means of sight.

Robert E. Ornstein explains, in *The Psychology of Consciousness* (1972:27), that our eyes are always active: "Our eyes are also constantly in motion, in large eye movements (saccades) as well as in eye tremors (nystagmus). We blink our eyes every second, move our eyes around, move our heads and bodies, and follow moving objects." The term *saccades* is French and means "the flick of a sail." Each saccade takes about one-twentieth of a second—the same amount of time needed to make possible *persistence of vision,* the process that enables us to connect the frames of a film and "see" the film as continuous.

When we scan a fixed image, our vision fades after a few seconds, and we sweep it again and again to signal our brains to keep the image in our minds; when we follow a moving object, our eyes follow it and keep it fixed on our retinas (Figure 1.4). What we describe as vision is a physiological process that involves light striking our retinas and becoming registered by photoreceptors located at the back of the retinas behind blood vessels and nerve fibers. This information is then processed by the brain. In the following excerpt, Ornstein suggests that we have to fashion an awareness out of the different inputs we get (1972:27).

▌ FIGURE 1.4
Scanning a "Nefertiti" postcard. The image on the left shows the saccades we make as we scan the sculpture of Nefertiti. Seeing involves a great deal of activity by our eyes, even though we are not aware of doing all this work.

If we "saw" an "image" on our retina, the visual world would be different each second, sometimes one object, then another, sometimes a blur due to the eyes moving, sometimes darkness due to blinks. We must then construct a personal consciousness from the selected input, and in this way achieve some stability of awareness out of the rich and continuously changing flow of information reaching our receptors.

That is, we must learn to select from all the information that is available to us and, in a sense, *construct* the world we see.

HEMISPHERES OF THE BRAIN

Our ability to process visual images seems to be related to our bicameral (two-hemisphered) brains. Research indicates that in normal people, even though both sides are involved in most activities, each hemisphere tends to specialize. Ornstein describes this phenomenon as follows (1972:51):

> The left hemisphere (connected to the right side of the body) is predominantly involved with analytic, logical thinking, especially in verbal and mathematical functions. Its mode of operation is primarily linear. This hemisphere seems to process information sequentially. . . . If the left hemisphere is specialized for analysis, the right hemisphere (again, remember, connected to the left side of the body) seems specialized for holistic mentation. This hemisphere is primarily responsible for our orientation in space, artistic endeavor, crafts, body image, recognition of faces.

As far as vision is concerned, both hemispheres of the brain play an important role.

Hanson (1987:41) tells us that while the left hemisphere is "more accurate in its ability to focus attention on something than is the right," the left side also tires more rapidly "and often gives way to the right." The right side maintains a general vigil in the surveillance of the environment, but it must call on the left hemisphere when it is necessary to pay attention to some detail.

When the right side does not call on the left side, a process that might be described as image *narcotization* takes place—a sense of monotony and boredom. On the other hand, using the left side of the brain is tiring, and so it must be reserved for occasions when focus and detail are important. Thus, both the left and right sides of the brain are needed, working in tandem, for people to process visual information in an optimal manner.

We can see the relationships that have been discussed in the chart that follows:

Left Hemisphere	*Right Hemisphere*
Right side of body	Left side of body
Analytical	Holistic
Logical	Artistic
Linear	Orientation in space
Sequential processing	Combinatory processing
Visual focus, detail	Surveillance, generalized vigil

With this in mind, we are prepared to consider our next topic, aesthetics.

AESTHETICS

Aesthetics means different things to different people. Courses in aesthetics, as it is conventionally understood, generally are offered by philosophy departments and tend to be theoretical in nature. Philosophers typically deal with *aesthetics* in terms of the following abstract questions.

▌ FIGURE 1.5
Gaston Lachaise, *Standing Woman (Heroic Woman)*, 1932, cast 1981. Does it make sense to ask whether you find this statue "beautiful," or is it better to ask how the artist achieved his desired effects? What effects does this statue have on you? How did the artist attain the effects he wanted?

1. What is the nature of the beautiful? (Consider the Lachaise sculpture in this respect; see Figure 1.5.)
2. What is the relationship between form and content?
3. Is beauty objective or subjective? Does it exist independent of our opinions, or is it mainly in the eye of the beholder, as some have suggested?

4. What is the relationship between truth and beauty?
5. What is the significance of ethical content? Need a work of art have moral value? If so, how do we define moral?
6. Should we consider the artist's intention in evaluating a work?

These questions are important, and we might bear them in mind as we proceed.

This book, however, is about *applied* aesthetics and focuses on the literal meaning of the term *aesthetics*, "space perception." The questions this book deals with are practical ones:

1. How do we obtain certain desired effects using the basic visual elements at our command?
2. How do we best exploit the powers (and deal with the limitations) of whatever medium we are working with?

In the world of applied aesthetics, we start with the *effect* we want and work backwards, using whatever we can to obtain that desired effect.

Taste is an important factor, of course, but it is very subjective. Taste is idiosyncratic; it is affected by factors such as sex, education, socioeconomic class, values, time, and culture. (Think, for example, how old-fashioned cars from the 1960s or fashions from just a few years back look today.) Some sociologists have suggested that there are "taste cultures" that shape the way people perceive things. From our perspective, that of applied aesthetics, taste reminds us that we must always know our audience and keep it in mind.

A PRIMER ON COMMUNICATION THEORY

Many theories and models have been developed that deal with communication theory—how people communicate with one another. One of the most famous models, created by the political scientist Harold Lasswell, asks:

Who?

Says what?

In which channel?

To whom?

With what effect?

Let me offer my own model, shown on the next page, which focuses on the relationships that exist among a work of art, the audience for whom it is intended, the medium used, the artist, and society. These are what I call the focal points, which can be used in the communication process.

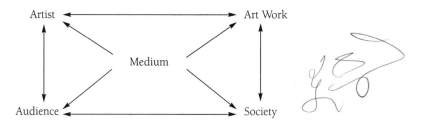

Focal Points in the Communication Process

The arrows in this model show that every focal point in the communication process is (or can be) connected to every other focal point.

Lasswell's and my model actually are very similar—except for the terminology—as the following chart shows:

Lasswell	Berger
Who?	Artist or sender
Says what?	Artwork
In which channel?	Medium used
To whom?	Audience or receiver
With what effect?	Social impact

Using Lasswell's model, we can understand communication to take place when someone says something (interpreted broadly), using some medium, to someone (including groups of people), with some effect.

For our purposes, let us consider the "effects" Lasswell mentions as being linked to the ability to understand (or, in technical terms, "decode") what has been said and have it generate some kind of impact—personal as well as social. For example, if I say something to you in Italian and you don't know Italian, it will simply be gibberish as far as you are concerned. Italian, here, is a code, and knowing Italian will enable you to decode my message. That is why icons are used in airports and other public places. They transmit messages by images, which most everyone can decode, and not by words—though iconic signs may use words as well.

The variations on this basic communication model are almost infinite in number and, in many cases, highly complex. Some models incorporate elements such as feedback or context or "two-step flows" between opinion leaders and the general public into their formulations. But the models discussed here offer us an overview of the most important elements in the communication process, a perspective that can easily be applied to visual communication.

THEORIES OF MORALITY

What is morality? Is an action right or wrong only in relation to certain conditions, or is it right or wrong independently of any conditions? Are the grounds for judging human conduct always the same, or should they vary with social and individual needs, customs, and historical evolution? Theories of morality may be classified as relativist or absolutist depending upon the answers they offer to these questions. But either relativism or absolutism may involve different general assumptions and may support different moral principles. An absolutist may argue for the invariant character of particular rules of conduct on the ground that they are di-vine commands, or that they are laws of nature, or that they are deducible from the concept of reason, or that they are intuitively self-evident. A relativist may hold that the rules of right conduct vary with human conventions, or with social traditions, or with political, psychological, economic, or biological needs. The history of ethical philosophy is a continuous dialogue between progressively more refined forms of absolutism and relativism.

Source: Raziel Abelson and Marie-Louise Friquegnon, *Ethics for Modern Life*, 4th ed. (New York: St. Martin's Press, 1991), 7.

ETHICS AND THE IMAGE

The power to create images, videos, films, commercials, television programs, and the like—all of which profoundly affect viewers' emotions and beliefs, and have social and cultural implications as well—should not be taken lightly. We must be ever mindful of our responsibilities toward those who will see what we create and, in many cases, believe what they see.

Even if people don't always believe what they see, or believe everything they see, they are often affected emotionally by the media to which they are exposed. For example, we know that professional wrestling is "fake," but people who watch it are still *viscerally* affected by seeing performers who are (or who seem to be) violently battering one another. Theater is "fake," too— actors and actresses pretend to have certain emotions and feelings. Audiences know this, but they still can be brought to tears in some cases or made to laugh hysterically in others.

Therefore, those who work in the media must consider their ethical responsibilities toward others. Ethics is, for our purposes, that branch of philosophy generally defined as dealing with "correct behavior," with what is "right" and what is "wrong." But what is "correct behavior"? What does it mean to act "morally" and avoid acting "immorally"? How do we know we're doing "the right thing" and avoiding doing "something wrong"?

Philosophers have debated ethics for thousands of years. Some philosophers have suggested that ethical behavior involves utilitarian considerations—"the greatest good for the greatest number." But how do we determine what the greatest good for the greatest number is?

Some philosophers argue that there are absolute standards of right and wrong. But others—the ethical relativists—argue that it is impossible to say, with any finality, that anything is *always* right or wrong. For example, in some societies, men have many wives, while in other societies, men have only one wife. Therefore, we cannot say conclusively that having more than one wife—or, by implication, doing anything else—is always right or always wrong.

CHECKLIST ON ETHICS AND THE MEDIA

Rather than dealing with ethics in terms of abstruse philosophical matters, let us operationalize our discussion and deal with some of the problems we face when we try to act in an ethical manner. Here are some key questions relating to ethical behavior for individuals who work with visual communication and other aspects of the media:

1. Will the works you create—videos, programs, commercials, print advertisements, and so on—give people distorted views of reality (to the extent that we can know reality, that is)?

2. Do your works use the power of images to exploit or manipulate people? Do your works attempt to get people to do things that are, or might be, self-destructive (like smoking cigarettes or drinking too much) or harmful to others?

3. Do your works stereotype people— members of racial or ethnic minorities or religious groups, for instance—and lead, as is often the case, to feelings of hatred toward and self-hatred by members of the stereotyped group?

4. Do your works have the power to disturb young viewers, who may not be emotionally able to deal with what they see?

5. Do your works contain gratuitous violence? Do they sexually exploit women's bodies? Are they sensationalistic?

6. Are your works something that you are not proud of? Do you have to rationalize your behavior by saying, "If I don't do it, someone else will . . . and I have responsibilities to my family as well"?

7. Do you create works you wouldn't want your children to see? If so, is it acceptable to create something that other people's children might see?

8. Do your works suggest some actions or values that you would be willing to universalize?

This last question reflects the ideas of the philosopher Immanuel Kant, who believed that ethical behavior should be based on what he called the "categorical imperative." Kant wrote in 1785: "Act as if the maxim of your action were to become through your will a universal law of nature." That is, I would suggest, a very good principle to keep in mind when considering the ethical responsibilities of individuals who work in the media.

Finally, many people believe we should obey the golden rule—"Do unto others as you would have them do unto you." But others have disagreed with that notion, saying, "Do not do unto others as you would have them do unto you—their tastes may not be the same as yours."

Deciding what's the right thing to do in any given situation is not easy, which explains why ethics is, and always has been, a very contentious branch of philosophy. But it is important for us to think, at all times, about ethics and the impact of what we do, not only for the good of society, but also for our own peace of mind.

CONCLUSIONS

Seeing Is Believing aims to entertain you (in the best sense of the term—namely, giving you ideas to "entertain"), as well as to teach you about visual communication, with the goal of helping you learn to see the world (and yourself) with more clarity and understanding.

APPLICATIONS

1. In order of importance, what visual phenomena are most important in shaping your identity? Consider such things as height, body shape, hair color, hairstyle, complexion, teeth, eye color, clothes, and so on.

2. List the most important status symbols in our culture. How do these symbols confer status on people? Is price the most important factor?

3. What makes a person "attractive"? Is beauty something that exists independent of people's opinion, or is it merely "in the eye of the beholder"?

4. It has been suggested that seeing isn't always believing—namely, that sometimes we are led astray by things we see. Give some examples of this. How can we use visual phenomena to deceive people?

5. In this discussion on aesthetics, a number of notions of what is most important in a work of art were mentioned: form, content, truthfulness, ethical qualities. Which of these concepts do you think is the critical one? What reasons can you offer to support your contention?

6. Aestheticians have suggested four theories of the purpose of art: (1) to generate emotional experiences in people, (2) to achieve certain consequences for individuals and society, (3) to mirror reality, and (4) to generate the artist's own reality. (These are known as the emotive, prag-

matic, mimetic, and objective theories of art, respectively.) Which of them strikes you as best? Why?

7. What is taste? Is taste a valid and useful means of evaluating works of art and other phenomena? If so, why? If not, why not?

8. Select some advertisements from fashionable and upscale magazines such as *Vogue* and *Architectural Digest* and middle-scale magazines such as *Better Homes and Gardens*. What differences do you notice in terms of such matters as the physical features of the models (male and female) in the advertisements? In the way men are shown relating to women? In the way women are portrayed?

9. Select some photographs or advertisements (with people in them) that reflect "beauty" in women and "handsomeness" in men. What do you find in common with selections made by your classmates? Have our definitions of beauty and handsomeness changed in recent years? If so, how do your photographs and advertisements reflect this? Are our definitions destructive? If so, how?

2

HOW WE SEE

Studies indicate that vision is about one-tenth physical and nine-tenths mental. In visual perception, sensory input in the form of light patterns received by the eye is transformed by the brain into meaningful images. The interpretation depends on preconditioning, intelligence, and the physical and emotional state of the viewer.

The variety of our responses to visual stimuli is demonstrated by artists. Twelve people depicting the same subject—even from the same vantage point—will create twelve different images because of their different experiences, attitudes, interests and eyesight.
 –DUANE AND SARAH PREBLE,
 ARTFORMS

This chapter deals with how we make sense of what we see. It introduces some basic principles of semiotics, or the science of signs, and some material from psychoanalytic theory, which can be used to help us understand how we find meaning in images and, by extension, in life, in general.

LEARNING TO SEE

The first thing we must recognize is that we don't just "see" but have to learn *how* to see and *what* to see. We cannot focus our attention on everything around us; somehow, we select certain things to look at. And what we decide to see is determined by what we know and what we believe and what we want. Consider our behavior in a supermarket, where we are surrounded by thousands of products, each clamoring for our attention. We "see" an estimated eight products every second that we're in the supermarket. We may try to neglect the products we feel we do not need or want—but it is very difficult for most people to avoid purchasing some products on the basis of "impulse." (More than 60 percent of all supermarket purchases are not planned in advance, which means that impulse buying is a major factor in our trips to the supermarket.) And it is primarily as a result of packaging— that is, the way products look—that we are attracted to them. We are also affected by the design of supermarkets and the placement of products on the shelves. If we have to stoop down or reach up to get a product, we are less likely to purchase it than if it is at eye level and easy to reach.

❚ FIGURE 2.1
Three renderings of fire. Our attitudes about fire are connected with everything from the myth of Prometheus (who stole fire from the gods and gave it to humans) to our beliefs about the existence of hell. What other images of fire can you think of?

The way we think about visual phenomena is affected by our knowledge. In *Ways of Seeing,* John Berger points out that in the Middle Ages, when people believed in the existence of hell, fire had a meaning much different from and more powerful than its current meaning (Figure 2.1).

We all have to be taught what different objects are (a plane, a ship, a dog, and so on, ad infinitum), but we learn so quickly and with so little effort that we generally don't recognize that a learning experience has taken place. We simply seem to pick up much of this information by osmosis. But the fact is, we do have to learn, and much of this learning involves visual phenomena.

There is a vast literature on visual matters—everything from highly abstract theoretical and philosophical treatises to experimental research studies. And in between are countless reports on applied research, on such topics as the way we perceive spaces or relate to colors, the responses generated by various kinds of film shots, the impact of editing, and the relationship between a medium and its message, to cite just a few.

We can't cover everything in this brief book, but by dealing with some of the most important aspects of visual communication, we can take that important first step on the "royal road" to visual understanding.

SIGNS, SYMBOLS, AND SEMIOTICS

How do we make sense of the visual world? Many of us never bother to think about this question because we do a pretty good job of interpreting the world around us and rarely reflect on *how* we know *what* we know.

Consider the following:

1. A drawing of a person (Figure 2.2)
2. A house with smoke coming out of a window (Figure 2.3)
3. A cross (Figure 2.4)

FIGURE 2.2
A very simple drawing of a man.

FIGURE 2.3
A house on fire. "Where there's smoke, there's fire."

FIGURE 2.4
A cross.

The list might go on endlessly: a photograph of a friend, a Rolls Royce, a flag, the Mona Lisa, the Eiffel Tower, the White House, the Pentagon, a Russian tank, a Big Mac, a computer, a great white shark, the Washington Monument, the Leaning Tower of Pisa, a football, and so on.

But how do we "make sense" of these three items?

In Figure 2.2, the matter is quite simple: the drawing looks like the person; and so we can say that drawings (as well as photographs, paintings, sculptures, and the like) communicate by *resemblance*. In Figure 2.3, we know from our experiences with fires—in fireplaces, at ceremonial events, in television news shows or films—that "where there's smoke, there's fire." Thus, we have good reason to believe that the smoke is *caused* by fire and that the building is on fire. In Figure 2.4, the cross is an object that we have *learned* is associated with Christianity and is an artifact having great resonance and emotional power for many Christians, because it symbolizes Christ's crucifixion. There is no way for a person to "naturally" know the meaning of a cross; there is no logical connection between the object and what it stands for the way there is between smoke and fire. (The connection is historical, not logical.)

Now let us consider another matter related to visual communication that we might add to the preceding list:

4. The word *tree*

The word *tree* and the object it refers to are shown in Figures 2.5 and 2.6. Linguists tell us that there is no natural connection between a word and the object it stands for. Thus, the word *tree* and the object it stands for (defined in *Webster's Ninth New Collegiate Dictionary* as a "woody perennial plant having a single, usually elongate main stem generally with few or no branches on the lower part") are not logically related. *The relationship between a word and the object it stands for is arbitrary or conventional.* This fact explains why dictionaries need to be revised all the time, because language is always changing. This same relationship between a word and its object also applies to all

FIGURE 2.5
The word *tree*.

FIGURE 2.6
A drawing of a tree.

kinds of other phenomena, in which we learn that something (a word, a facial expression, an object, a hairstyle) signifies or stands for something else.

Let's recapitulate. We make sense of visual phenomena in a number of ways:

1. *Resemblance* (as in photographs)
2. *Cause and effect* or *logic* (as in smoke implying fire)
3. *Convention* (as in objects that have symbolic value)
4. *Signification* (as in a smile signifying pleasure)

There is a science that is of great utility in helping us understand how visual phenomena communicate—a field of knowledge called semiotics, the science of signs. Two theories are encompassed here: one is the field known as semiotics, which was developed by the American philosopher C. S. Peirce, and the other is the field known as semiology, developed by the Swiss linguist Ferdinand de Saussure. For the sake of simplicity, we'll use the term *semiotics* to cover both of these theories.

What Signs Are

A sign, from the semiotic perspective, is anything that stands for something else. What does this statement mean? Only that a great deal of communication is done not directly but rather indirectly, by using various signs. For instance, there are several ways to suggest that an actor is portraying a secret agent (Figure 2.7). The actor could say, "I am a secret agent," or a narrator could tell us. Or the actor could wear a trench coat and a slouch hat, carry a small revolver with a silencer, and drive a fast sports car. All of these are signs that, taken together, suggest a secret agent.

ICONS, INDEXES, AND SYMBOLS. Peirce identifies three kinds of signs: iconic, indexical, and symbolic, as the chart on the following page shows. An *icon* is a sign that looks like or resembles the thing it stands for—which means that icons are easy to interpret; the drawing in Figure 2.2 is an icon. Because icons are so easy to interpret, signs in airports are often icons—pictures that most people, regardless of the language they speak, should be able to understand. An *indexical sign* is logically connected to what it represents; in Figure 2.3, smoke indicates fire. We have to learn about this connection and do so, often, simply from everyday life. A *symbol*, on the other hand, has conventional meaning, and there is no logical connection between this meaning and the symbol itself. It is something we have to learn, as with the cross in Figure 2.4. We can see the relation that exists among icons, indexes, and symbols in the chart that follows.

▌ FIGURE 2.7
Ways to suggest a secret agent.

	Icon	Index	Symbol
Signify by	Resemblance	Causal connection	Convention
Examples	Photograph	Smoke/fire	Cross or flag
Process	Can recognize	Can figure out	Must learn

Peirce's theory is actually very involved, but these three central concepts can help us to understand visual communication. For example, internists and other "cognitive" physicians (in contrast to surgeons and other "operative" physicians) work on the basis of indexical knowledge. They see various signs, and patients tell them about their symptoms; and on the basis of these phenomena, they try to determine what is causing a problem. All of us recognize the power symbols have over people—flags, the crucifix, the Star of David, college banners, logos . . . one could go on endlessly. These symbols can generate enormously powerful emotional responses in people. In fact, people often are willing to give their lives for the institutions and organizations behind these symbols.

Peirce notes that "the universe is perfused with signs, if not made up entirely of them," which means that *everything can be seen as a sign of something else* and that human beings are sign-producing and sign-analyzing beings. *Logos* are designs that are used to stand for and help reinforce the identity of a corporation or other entity (Figures 2.8 and 2.9). If everything in the universe is a sign or can be understood as one, it certainly makes sense to learn how to interpret and understand signs.

The situation becomes more complex because the boundaries between icon, index, and symbol are often vague. As Sandra E. Moriarty explains in "Abduction: A Theory of Visual Interpretation" (1996:169):

▌ FIGURE 2.8
Logos for Saturn motorcars. Of these four versions, the first one was chosen. All offer somewhat different "images" for the automobile, and all contain pictorial references to the planet Saturn.

■ **FIGURE 2.9**

These portraits enable us to see how Betty Crocker's image has evolved over the years, from her introduction in 1936 to the present. As a pamphlet produced by General Mills explains, a nationwide search identified 75 women of different backgrounds and ages who embodied the characteristics of Betty Crocker. Then "a computerized composite of the 75 women, along with the 1986 portrait of Betty, served as inspiration for the painting by the internationally known artist John Stuart Ingle."

A rose can be an icon (a picture), an index (a sign of summer), and a symbol (the War of the Roses). Photographs are indexical as well as iconic because they are reality grounded. In communication production and reception, the meaning may shift from one to another as the communication act progresses. For example, Sinead O'Connor's iconoclastic tearing up of the picture of Pope John Paul II . . . illustrates how conflict can be generated when an iconic representation is turned into a symbol.

An iconoclast is, literally, a destroyer or breaker of icons—but generally refers to someone who is unconventional and who goes against the grain as well as someone who destroys sacred icons. We see, then, that applying Peirce's ideas can be quite complicated.

SIGNIFIERS AND SIGNIFIEDS. The second theory, Saussure's, argues that a sign is divided into two parts: a signifier and a signified. A *signifier* is defined by Saussure as a sound or object that calls to mind a concept or *signified* (Figures 2.10 and 2.11). According to Saussure, the relationship that exists between the signifier and signified is arbitrary or conventional—that is, the relationship is not natural but must be learned.

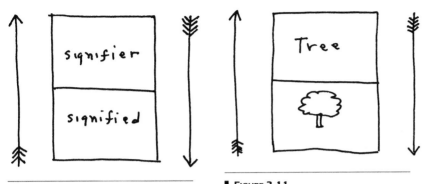

■ FIGURE 2.10
Signifier / signified diagram.

■ FIGURE 2.11
Signifier / signified diagram for tree.

Therefore, in Saussure's view, no signifier—whether a word or a drawing or any other kind of sign—is self-explanatory and implies a specific signified. A given facial expression—a wink, for example—can mean a number of different things, depending on the situation. As the semiotic theorists often point out, if signs can be used to tell the truth, they also can be used to lie.

Saussure makes another extremely important point. He notes that concepts don't mean anything on their own; they are always defined in terms of how they differ from other concepts. As he puts it (1966:117), "Concepts are purely differential and defined not by their positive content but negatively by their relations with the other terms in the system."

Meaning, then, is determined not by content but by relationships. As Saussure (1966:117) suggests, as far as concepts are concerned, "their most precise characteristic is in being what the others are not." This explains why our thinking tends to be so binary, so connected to oppositions—because that's the way language requires us to make sense of things.

This idea about concepts generating meaning relationally has significance in a number of areas when it comes to visual communication. We will see, for example, that a color's impact depends to a great degree on the colors around it. And size, as we all recognize, is also relative. With this in mind, let us consider what signs can do.

What Signs Can Do

Let's look at several examples of how signs can mean different things and how we can use them for a variety of purposes. For one thing, we can lie with signs. People who dye their hair are, from this perspective, "lying" with signs—though this kind of lying is not considered of great consequence. People who lease expensive cars and represent themselves as the owner are, in a sense, lying with signs (or, in this case, status symbols). When we laugh at a joke that we have heard before so that we don't embarrass the joke teller, we are lying. Or are we merely being polite?

No sign, when some kind of a sign is expected, is also a kind of sign. If you say hello to a friend and don't get a response, that is a sign. Not doing something when something is expected of you is a kind of sign for a behavior known as "aggressive passivity"; in other words, doing nothing or not responding can, in certain situations, be seen as a form of aggressive behavior. This "aggressive passivity" or "passive aggression" is often used by children to "get back" at their parents—for example, by taking forever to do their chores.

Signs are used by people as a means of getting information and drawing conclusions about things. During the Iran-Contra hearings of 1987, commentators made much of the participants' facial expressions and body language, as a means of trying to understand what the participants *really* felt or believed. In the case of William Casey, the late CIA director, however, this was impossible, because Casey was "stone faced." Furthermore, the president, Ronald Reagan, had an extensive background in acting, and actors are people who can pretend to have feelings and beliefs that they don't really have.

Codes

Because the relationship that exists between signs and what they mean (from Saussure's perspective) is arbitrary, we have to find ways of making sense of signs; we do so via codes. *Codes* can be looked at as ways of making sense of signs, as systems of conventions that we are taught or pick up from our culture. In fact, what we know as culture in anthropological terms can be seen as a collection of codes.

In some cases, these codes are created and systematized—as in the driving codes that we all must learn in order to get a license. These codes are collections of rules that tell us what to do when we see certain signs and when we find ourselves in particular situations. Thus, we learn that when we see a red light we must stop our cars, and when we see a green one we can accelerate or continue on if we have not stopped.

These codes list the conventions we have adopted in order to make it possible for us to get from one place to another with the minimum of danger and confusion. Figure 2.12 shows some of the visual signs and symbols used on roads and highways. Some of these signs are iconic, and we can make sense of them without having to be taught what they mean. But others are symbolic and conventional, and we must learn what they mean. In some cases, we have redundancy, in which a message is repeated in several ways to reinforce its impact.

These driving codes and others like them are one kind of code. They are really collections of laws and rules. There are other kinds of codes, however, that are learned more or less by osmosis as people grow up in a particular culture. These involve the whole universe of beliefs (many of which exist at a level below awareness or articulation) that tell us what things mean or what to do in given situations.

For example, we have certain ideas about what being a "blonde" means, about what having a weak chin means, about what having "shifty" eyes means, about what being short or tall or fat or skinny means. We have notions about what certain kinds of food mean and when to eat them. For instance, in the United States, we eat salad before the main course, while in France and other European countries, the salad is generally eaten after the main course. (What we call culture shock is generally the result of finding ourself in a society where the codes or culture-codes are different from what one is used to.) We have notions of how to dress for job interviews and what certain styles, colors, and fashions mean. We should recognize here that it is also possible to misinterpret signs. Because of differences in education, region, class, and so on, people often interpret (or *decode*, to use the semiotic term) signs in widely varying ways. This aberrant decoding is a problem for people—such as writers, artists, filmmakers, and especially those who create commercials and print advertisements—who try to convey something to people but find those people interpreting it in unanticipated ways.

▌ FIGURE 2.12
Road signs use icons or language, and sometimes both, to convey their messages. Note the simplicity of the drawings in the signs.

Metaphors and Metonymies

Many of these codes are connected to visual matters, as we've already suggested. And much of what we know or think we know from observing various visual signs is based on associations we make or have been taught to make about signs and what they signify. The technical term for these associations is *metonymy*. An example of this phenomenon would be an advertise-

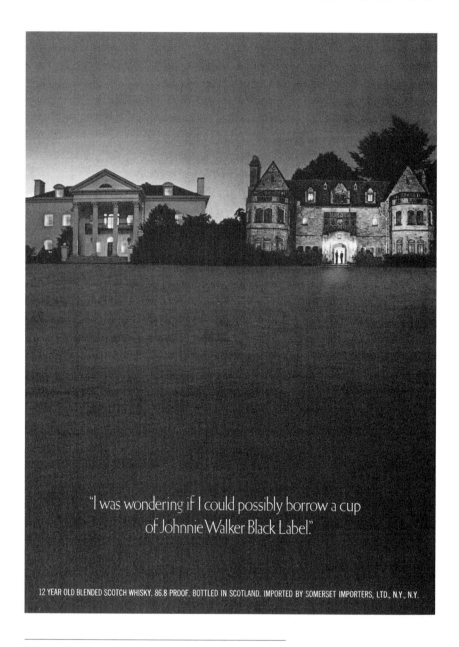

"I was wondering if I could possibly borrow a cup of Johnnie Walker Black Label."

12 YEAR OLD BLENDED SCOTCH WHISKY. 86.8 PROOF. BOTTLED IN SCOTLAND. IMPORTED BY SOMERSET IMPORTERS, LTD., N.Y., N.Y.

▍ FIGURE 2.13
Johnnie Walker advertisement. This advertisement uses the association (metonymy) of wealth and elegance to suggest sophistication and quality.

ment for Scotch whisky that shows the liquor being used by people who live in a mansion and are obviously rich and—it is suggested—have good taste. We learn to associate that brand of Scotch with what might be called "high-class" people and upscale living. The advertisement in Figure 2.13 is an example of the use of metonymy or association. Advertising makes great use of the power of *association* because this technique conveys information quickly and powerfully.

Another important method of transmitting meaning involves using *analogies*—saying or suggesting that something is like or similar to something else. Consider the two statements that follow:

1. My love *is* a red rose.
2. My love *is like* a red rose.

In the first case, we are making a very strong kind of analogy and are, in fact, suggesting equivalence. This figure of speech is known as a *metaphor.* In the second case, we are suggesting that our love is similar to a red rose, a figure of speech known as a *simile.* In both cases, the meaning is created by making an analogy.

Some scholars argue that metaphor is the basic way we have of knowing about the world and that human thinking is itself essentially metaphoric. As George Lakoff and Mark Johnson have written in *Metaphors We Live By* (1980:3):

> Metaphor is typically viewed as a characteristic of language alone, a matter of words rather than thought or action. For this reason, most people think they can get along perfectly well without metaphor. We have found, on the contrary, that metaphor is pervasive in everyday life, not just in language but in thought and action. Our ordinary conceptual system, in terms of which we both think and act, is fundamentally metaphorical in nature.
>
> The concepts that govern our thoughts are not just matters of the intellect. They also govern our everyday functioning down to the most mundane details. Our concepts structure what we perceive, how we get around in the world, and how we relate to other people. Our conceptual system thus plays a central role in defining our everyday reality.

Thus, metaphors play a central role in our thinking about the world and our functioning in it. The metaphors we have shape, it could be argued, our conception of the world and our place in it.

If, for example, you think that "love is a game" or that "love is like a game," certain logical implications will follow. You will see love as essentially a contest, with winners and losers and rules (that can be broken, in certain circumstances), and as something that ends after a certain period of "playing." This hardly seems a healthy or satisfying way to think about love.

I FIGURE 2.14
Here is a visual metaphor
that you might find
amusing.

Metaphor and simile are not confined to words and written language—they are also part of our visual language and pervade our image making (Figure 2.14). For example, in the comics, the Spiderman costume is a visual analogy; so is the characterization of Newt Gingrich as a "bomb" in *Doonesbury*. Freud's notion of "phallic and vaginal symbols," which will be discussed later, is based on visual analogies. Because metaphor and metonymy play such an important role in communication, it is only logical to find them in pictorial form as well as in our words.

It is not unusual for a given sign or symbol to have both metonymic and metaphoric aspects to it; that is, to communicate by using both associations and analogies.

Think, for example, of our old friend, the snake. We, in the West, *associate* the snake with Adam and Eve in the Garden of Eden and with our eating from the Tree of Knowledge and being expelled from Eden. Thus, the snake is connected, in Western minds familiar with the Old Testament, with deception ("The serpent beguiled me," Eve says) and a host of other negative things like having to work and having to die. At the same time, snakes are long and thin (which means their shape makes them resemble penises), and thus, they are *analogous* to or function as phallic symbols. (In certain Eastern countries, on the other hand, the fact that snakes shed their skins and become "new" again leads people to associate snakes with rebirth and immortality.)

There's a wonderful example of visual metaphors in Chapter 4 of *Alice in Wonderland*. Alice's neck has stretched out very long, and a pigeon who sees her thinks she is a snake:

"Serpent!" screamed the Pigeon.
  "I'm *not* a serpent!" said Alice indignantly. "Let me alone!"
  "Serpent, I say again!" repeated the Pigeon, but in a more subdued tone, and added, with a kind of sob, "I've tried every way but nothing seems to suit them!"

The Pigeon describes how she's hidden her eggs in many different places but has not been able to keep them from the serpents. Alice takes issue with her:

"But I'm *not* a serpent, I tell you!" said Alice. "I'm a—I'm a—"
  "Well! *What* are you?" said the Pigeon. "I can see you're trying to invent something."
  "I—I'm a little girl," said Alice, rather doubtfully, as she remembered a number of changes she had gone through that day.
  "A likely story indeed!" said the Pigeon, in a tone of deepest contempt. "I've seen a good many little girls in my time, but never *one* with such a neck as that! No, No! You're a serpent; and there's no use denying it. I suppose you'll be telling me next that you've never tasted an egg!"

"I *have* tasted eggs, certainly," said Alice, who was a very truthful child; "but little girls eat eggs quite as much as serpents do, you know."

"I don't believe it," said the Pigeon; "but if they do, why, then they're a kind of serpent: that's all I can say."

For the Pigeon, the fact that Alice is a creature with an extremely elongated neck who admits to eating eggs is enough to classify her as a serpent, an interpretation that is visually metaphoric and, in the realm of ideas, metonymic.

The following chart summarizes the differences between metaphor and metonymy, as well as their subcategories, simile and synecdoche.

Metaphor	*Metonymy*
Analogy	Association
Meta = transfer, beyond	*Meta* = transfer, beyond
phor = to bear, carry	*onoma* = name
Love is a game	Rolls Royce = wealth
Simile uses *like* or *as*	*Synecdoche* uses part for whole or whole for part
Love is *like* a game	The Pentagon (for U.S. military)
Alice looks *like* a snake	Alice eats eggs

Obviously, it is very difficult to communicate anything with precision and certainty, because signs are so open to interpretation and misinterpretation and convey their information in so many different ways.

Condensation and Displacement

To further complicate matters, we must understand something about how the mind processes signs and symbols and other visual phenomena. Think of your dreams, for instance. In your dreams, you see all kinds of fantastic things. Sometimes, you see several different things tied together in bizarre ways. You might see a train with wings or a building floating in water. In dreams, the mind, for its own reasons, unifies disparate phenomena and creates fantastic images.

The Bible is full of dreams and visions that feature incredible images and about which there is still much controversy. Consider, for example, the famous vision of the prophet Ezekiel (Ezek. 1.1):

And I looked, and behold, a whirlwind came out of the north, a great cloud, and a fire infolding itself, and a brightness was about it, and out of the midst thereof as the color of amber, out of the midst of the fire. Also out of the midst thereof came the likeness of four living creatures. And this was their appearance; they had the likeness of man. And every one had four faces, and every one had four wings. And their feet were straight feet; and the sole of their feet was like the sole of a calf's foot; and they sparkled like the color of burnished brass. And they had the hands of a man under their wings on their four sides . . . As for the likeness of their faces, the four had the face of a man, and the face of a lion, on the right side, and the four had the face of an ox on the left side; the four also had the face of an eagle.

The process by which we combine elements of various signs together to form a new composite sign or symbol is called *condensation.* In another important process, called *displacement,* we transfer meaning from one sign or symbol to another, so that, for example, a rifle or a plane really stands for a phallus (if you understand what is going on and know how to interpret such matters).

These terms come to us from Freud, who discussed them in his classic book, *The Interpretation of Dreams.* He used the terms to explain how the psyche uses images to evade what he termed the *dream censor* and avoid being wakened. By condensing images or displacing content from one image to something else, we "trick" the dream censor, so to speak. In many cases, these condensations and displacements involve sexual matters. These two techniques enable us, then, to have our sexual fantasies and, by disguising them and fooling the dream censor, to avoid being wakened.

These terms are important because much of what we find in visual phenomena involves the use of these processes, and, as in dreams, much visual communication takes place at the unconscious level. And these processes also are connected to profoundly important unconscious matters in our psyches, which explains why so many visual phenomena have the emotional impact that they do. Symbols carry a great deal of emotional baggage, on both a cultural and a personal level, and have the power to evoke powerful, and often unrecognized, responses in us.

What Freud has described as phallic symbols—rifles, umbrellas, knives, and other objects similar to a phallus in shape and function—are really good examples of displacements. Our society does not allow us to show male and female genitalia in print advertisements, for example, but it is possible (and often done, many argue) to use phallic symbols that evade the censors and call to mind various aspects of our sexuality. Consider here the symbolic significance of the monument for George Washington, the father of our country, being a large phallic shaft stretching up into the sky (Figure 2.15).

Surrealistic styles, which unite all kinds of disparate phenomena, are examples of condensation in action (Figure 2.16). And the power of surrealistic styles (found often on MTV) stems from the psychological associations connected with the various signs and symbols pulled together.

❚ FIGURE 2.15
Washington Monument.

▌ FIGURE 2.16
What is this cow doing in this man's bed? This image, taken from *L'Age d'Or,* is typical of surrealism's use of fantastic images and strange incongruities that imitate dreams to express the workings of the human unconscious mind.

As the various paintings, advertisements, and other works reproduced in this book show, we generally find signs existing in some kind of context that includes other signs and symbols. This combination of signs and symbols is what we commonly describe as an image.

THE IMAGE

From our perspective, *an image is a collection of signs and symbols*—what we find when we look at a photograph, a film still, a shot of a television screen, a print advertisement, or just about anything. The word can also be used to mean a number of other things, including a mental representation we have of something, such as "the image of the businessman in nineteenth-century American literature."

Images generally are visual, often are mediated—carried by the mass media—and are connected to information, values, beliefs, attitudes, and ideas people have. This connection is not a natural one, remember; we have to learn to interpret many signs and symbols, which are important component elements of images. An image is a collection of signs, and each of these signs has meaning; in any image, there are many different levels of meaning and interactions between meanings.

Think of an advertisement in which a man is shown smiling and drinking a stein of frosty beer in a tavern; from his facial expression, he seems to be having a good time. In this image (which may be accompanied by words), the bubbles in the beer, the frost on the stein, the foam, and the smile all are signs meant to convey information and generate certain attitudes in the minds of viewers.

Images, of course, do not come into existence of their own volition. They are generally created and mediated—meant to be seen and read and to have a specific function and impact. Let us now consider how images relate to media, creators, audiences, and society in general. Using the focal points model discussed earlier, we can focus on images in terms of the following elements:

1. The *artists,* who create images
2. The *audience,* which receives images
3. The *work of art,* which is an image itself and might comprise a number of images
4. The *society* in which the images are found
5. The *medium,* which affects the images

A complex interaction of these five factors makes the way images work difficult to describe. The artists or creators of the images try to use signs that the audience will interpret or decode correctly; in this case, "correctly" means the way the artists want them to. The image itself is affected by the medium in which it is found, by various artistic conventions in a given medium (for example, television is often held to be a medium dependent on "close-ups" due to the small screen), and by the audience to which the image is directed. Signs and symbols such as Uncle Sam or the Republican Elephant also often have historical significance that may be recognized by some people and not by others. These signs may allude to important cultural, political, historical, and social experiences that a stranger in the society might not recognize or understand (Figure 2.17). Because of all these complications, communicating anything clearly and unambiguously is difficult. These factors also make our communications powerful and even put them beyond the control of those who create signs and symbols. It might be suggested that communication often takes place between the unconscious of the creators—the artists— and the unconscious of the receivers—the audience—so that the situation becomes even more mixed up. Nobody, in such a situation, completely understands or fully appreciates what is being communicated and what impact it is having.

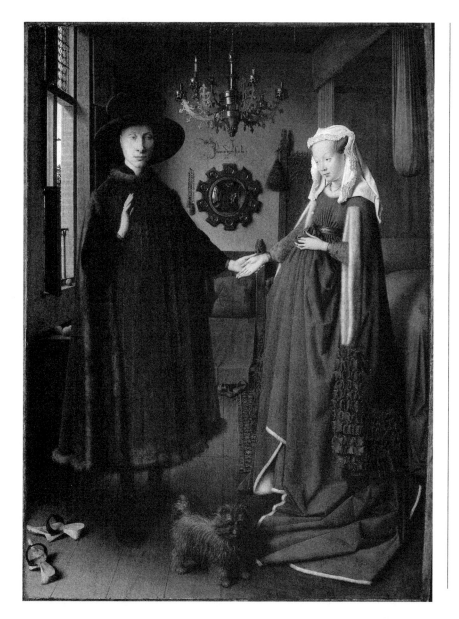

▌FIGURE 2.17

Jan van Eyck, *Giovanni Arnolfini and His Bride*, 1434. Many of the symbols used in this painting were understood in van Eyck's time but are not generally recognized now. Thus, the lighted candle in the chandelier signifies Christ's presence and the ardor of the newlyweds as well; the convex mirror suggests the eye of God seeing everything and seems to reflect the painter and another witness; the dog symbolizes marital faithfulness; the bride has her hand on her stomach (and appears to be pregnant), signifying her willingness to have children; the fruit is tied to symbolism connected with the Virgin Mary; the carving in the back of the chair is of Saint Margaret, the patron saint of childbirth; and the shoes are probably an allusion to the commandment by God to Moses to take off his shoes when on sacred soil. The signature of the painting and the date are also prominent, to record this event. When looking at a painting or any image of a symbolic nature, what we know determines how fully we can understand and interpret it.

One thing is certain—images do have powerful emotional effects on people. Your self-image, for example, affects the perceptions others have of you; and their perceptions, in turn, affect the image you have of yourself. It is not unusual for people to change their images over the years and create new "identities" for themselves, as they move through their life cycles and find themselves in new situations. A person might be a hippie in his twenties, wear three-piece suits and be a "buttoned-down" businessman in his forties, and become a priest or rabbi in his sixties—three major changes in identity (and "look") in one lifetime.

Images often have a historical significance. The meaning a given image has may also change over time, as a society develops and changes its views about things. Images also play an important role in religion and the arts. Think of the importance of visual elements in our religious ceremonies, in which we find people performing certain ritual activities, wearing certain costumes, using certain artifacts, and doing so in a space full of signs and symbols. The lighting is often important in such ceremonies, because it helps generate specific attitudes—such as a feeling of awe or piety or mystery.

To see how the various aspects of images work, examine the following chart, which summarizes much of the discussion made to this point.

DECODING VISUAL COMMUNICATION

Concept	Example	Method
Icon	Photograph	Resemblance
Index	Smoke from window	Cause and effect
Symbol	Crucifix	Convention
Signifier and signified	Bowler hat = Englishness	Convention
Condensation	Face/automobile	Unification
Displacement	Rifle = penis	Substitution
Metaphor	Spiderman's costume	Analogy
Metonymy	Huge mansion = wealth	Association

OPTICAL AND HAPTICAL WAYS OF SEEING

Another theorist whose ideas are of interest here is the art historian Alois Riegl. He suggests that there are two opposing ways of seeing things, the *optical* and the *haptical*. His ideas are explained in Claude Gandelman's *Reading Pictures, Viewing Texts* (1991:5) as follows:

> The two fundamental categories . . . are optics and haptics. Riegl stated that one type of artistic procedure, which corresponds to a certain way of looking, is based on the scanning of objects according to their outlines. This trajectory Riegl called the optical. The opposite type of vision, which focuses on surfaces and emphasizes the value of the superficies of objects, Riegl called the haptical (from the Greek *haptein,* "to seize, grasp," or *haptikos,* "capable of touching"). On the level of artistic creation, the optical look—if the eye belongs to a painter—pro-

duces linearity and angularity, whereas haptic creativity focuses on surfaces. Using Riegl's formula, all forms of art may be grouped under the heading "outline and/or color in plane or volume." . . . The optical eye merely brushes the surface of things. The haptic, or tactile, eye penetrates in depth, finding its pleasure in texture and grain.

The following chart (to which I've added some other relevant material from Gandelman) summarizes the differences between the two categories of seeing.

Optical	Haptical
Surface	Depth penetration
Scans outline	Sees texture, grain
Linear	Pictorial
Metaphoric	Metonymic

Gandelman sees the optical as metaphoric because, with that kind of viewing, one scans an object and establishes relationships among elements that aren't necessarily in contact with one another. The haptical can be seen as metonymic because it tends to focus attention on selected elements of an object (its color, grain, and so on), that is, on a part of the object rather than the whole object.

Interestingly, Gandelman argues, using Riegl's theory, that we also "view" literary texts (we scan them, with our eyes jumping from one passage to another) the same way we look at paintings and that we "read" paintings and other kinds of graphic art much the way we read books. This observation explains Gandelman's title: *Reading Pictures, Viewing Texts*. Note that the term *text* is conventionally used by critics to mean a work of art—in any medium. That is why critics often talk about "reading television" or "reading films," suggesting that television programs and films can be "read" and analyzed just as poems or novels are. The key is simply knowing the "language" these texts are "written" in—which is, to a considerable degree, the subject of this book.

CONCLUSIONS

In this chapter, we examined some of the complications involved in "seeing." It is not automatic, and we don't see without doing some thinking to make sense of what we see. We see selectively, focusing our attention on sights that interest us and paying little attention to ones that don't. This is necessary, because if we paid the same amount of attention to every visual stimulus, we'd never get very much done.

APPLICATIONS

1. Applying your knowledge of semiotics, assume you are a television director and wish to give your viewers information and elicit certain feelings without using words. What visual phenomena—that is, what images—would you show on the screen to generate the following concepts: horror, terror, secret agent, "Frenchness," love, hate, alienation? Choose some other concepts as well. Remember, also, that sometimes the combination of visual images helps generate the concept.

2. Bring any small, simple object that you think reflects your personality to class in a brown paper bag and give it to your instructor. (This is to prevent people from knowing who brought what.) Write your name on the bottom of the bag and list the attributes the object has that you expect your classmates to find. Do your classmates interpret things correctly, or do they see things that surprise you? What do you learn from this exercise?

3. Analyze a full-page color advertisement containing people and words in terms of the various signs found in it. (Remember that words are signs also.) What signs do you find? How do they work? Do you detect any codes functioning? If so, what are they, and how do they work? (You can also use some of the advertisements reprinted in this book.)

4. Write down a dream you had in as much detail as you can. Using Freud's notions of displacement and condensation, how do you analyze the dream? If you are interested in the Jungian analysis of dreams, read Jung's *Man and His Symbols* and use his concepts to analyze the same dream.

5. Look through a magazine and find examples of linguistic and visual metaphors and metonymies (and similes and synecdoches) in advertisements. What role do you think these devices play in the advertisements?

6. Take a logo for some company and, using what you've learned about visual semiotics, redesign the logo. How does your logo work, and why is it superior to the logo the company has been using?

ELEMENTS OF VISUAL COMMUNICATION

BASIC ELEMENTS

We are now ready to consider some of the fundamental elements found in visual communication. We'll start with the most basic unit, the dot.

Dots

The first element in analyzing visual phenomena is the *dot,* a small circular point in space. Dots can be used to indicate lines and thus shapes (Figure 3.1). An interesting phenomenon occurs when we see three dots that are not in a straight line. As Gaetano Kanitza explains in *The Mind's Eye* (1986:82):

> When we view three dots that are equidistant from one another and are not in a straight line, the visual system spontaneously organizes the dots into a triangle. In addition the three dots appear to be connected by straight lines. These lines

▋ FIGURE 3.1
Dots. Dots can be combined in various ways to form lines, and these lines can be used to create shapes.

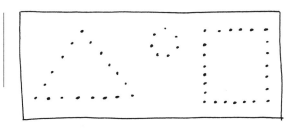

The fovea is a small circular pit in the center of the retina containing roughly 25,000 closely packed color-sensitive cones, each with its own nerve fiber. . . . In man, needle-threading, removal of splinters, and engraving are some of the many activities made possible by foveal vision. . . .

Surrounding the fovea is the macula, an oval, yellow body of color-sensitive cells. . . . [T]he cells are not as closely packed as they are in the fovea. Among other things man uses the macula for reading.

The man who detects movement out of the corner of his eye is seeing peripherally. Moving away from the central portion of the retina, the character and quality of vision change radically. The ability to see color diminishes as the color-sensitive cones become more scattered. . . .

– EDWARD HALL
THE HIDDEN DIMENSION

51

are called virtual, and although they are not actually seen, they are a real presence in our visual experience.

Thus, dots can be used to create virtual shapes as well as actual ones. And, of course, when we watch television, we are actually watching dots or *pixels* (picture elements), which are used to create images—much the same way that the pointillist artist Georges Seurat did.

We are now ready to move on to the next element—the line—which has been described as "a dot that went for a walk."

Lines

A succession of these dots or points in which the dots are not distinguishable forms a *line,* one of the basic elements found in visual phenomena. We use lines to indicate what things look like and what their shape is. Lines are sometimes formed on their own, but they are also formed as the edge of shapes.

Kanitza points out that "subjective contours" are formed by certain combinations of incomplete figures. Just as our visual system supplies lines between three equidistant dots, it also generates shapes. As we see in Figure 3.2, the visual system creates a "whiter-than-white" subjective triangle. This works only if we look at the figure as a whole; if we examine parts of it, the triangle disappears. Psychologists are extremely interested in the way our eyes play tricks on us and have done extensive research on optical illusions and related topics.

When we look at actual lines in drawings and other works of art, we find that artists often develop distinctive "lines." We can see this in the work of cartoonists; some use a smooth, liquid, delicate line, while others favor a heavy, rough line. Thus, lines can have their own qualities and generate varying responses.

▌ Figure 3.2
The cutouts in the three circles, which look like the corners of a triangle, inevitably lead the eye to create a subjective or imaginary triangle in the mind's eye.

Shapes

Lines can be generated, more or less indirectly, from shapes; but they also can create *shapes*—in outline form. According to Donis A. Dondis, in *A Primer of Visual Literacy,* there are three basic shapes: the *triangle* (an object made from three lines), the *square* (an object made from four lines of equal length at right angles to one another), and the *circle* (a figure in which all points in the circumference are equidistant from the center point) (Figure 3.3). All other shapes or figures can be thought of as being variations on

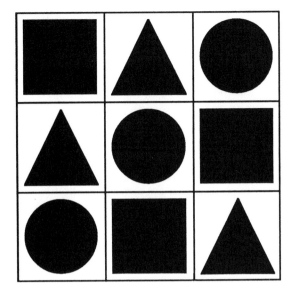

these three basic shapes. Dondis suggests that these three basic shapes have their own character (1973:44):

> Each of the basic shapes has its own unique character and characteristics and to each is attached a great deal of meaning, some through association, some through arbitrary attached meaning, and some through our own psychological and physiological perceptions. The square has associated to it dullness, honesty, straightness, and workmanlike meaning; the triangle, action, conflict, tension; the circle, endlessness, warmth, protection.

Shapes, then, by themselves, have the power to generate certain feelings and responses.

In some cases, shapes are created by forming lines; but in other cases, shapes are formed as the result of other phenomena. Think, for example, of the *figure-ground* relationship—the relationship between an object and the background against which we see the object—and the famous problem it presents to our minds. Figure 3.4 shows a drawing of two faces in profile *or*

❙ FIGURE 3.4
Figure-ground representation. One can see either the faces or the vase, but not both together at the same time.

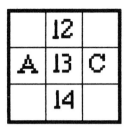

▌ FIGURE 3.5
This figure shows the importance of context in interpreting visual phenomena. Many images are somewhat ambiguous and depend on the context in which they are found for meaning. Reading down, the image in the center block is the number 13; reading across, it is the letter B.

of a vase, depending on how we look at it. What is important to recognize is that it is impossible to see *both* the profiles and the vase at the same time. We can see either the vase or the profiles, that is, either the figure or the ground.

This figure-ground concept is important in other cases, for we often find that the ground, or context, helps determine the meaning of a figure or object, in the same way that the context in which a word is found often helps us understand how the word is meant to be understood (Figure 3.5). Thus, for example, a syringe can suggest drug abuse or medical applications, depending on whether the syringe is seen in a "shooting gallery" or a hospital.

Volume

If we think of shape as a two-dimensional figure (length and width), then when we move into a third dimension—depth—we get an object, something that has *volume*. Our eyes are used to a world where objects have volume, and most of the visual phenomena we are involved with have volume—or seem to. A drawing of a building is a two-dimensional figure that tricks the eye into thinking it is seeing something in three dimensions (Figure 3.6).

Scale

Scale refers to relationships in size between shapes and objects. Unless we have a scale of reference, we cannot know how large or small something is just by seeing it. If, for example, we see a drawing of a human figure, we immediately can set the scale, because people tend to be between five and six feet tall (Figure 3.7).

▌ FIGURE 3.6
This drawing suggests volume by adding depth to the dimensions of length and width.

ANT   HUMAN   HUMAN   MOUNTAIN

❚ **FIGURE 3.7**
Scale. Scale is a concept based on some kind of a comparison. Thus, a human being is gigantic relative to an ant but insignificant relative to a mountain.

Semiotics tells us, in fact, that concepts have no meaning in themselves; they make sense only because they have some relationship to some other concept (most often their opposite). In the same way, shapes and objects are indeterminate in size until placed into a relationship with some other shape or object whose size is known.

Scale carries emotional impact. The feelings we have when we are in a small room are different from those we have when we are in a gigantic space where we are "dwarfed" and seem insignificant.

Spatiality

Our discussion of scale leads to the concept of *spatiality,* an important element in pictorial design. We have learned to associate large, open spaces with wealth and class and small, cramped spaces with the opposite; perhaps this association comes from the mansions and estates in which the wealthy live. Thus, the way space is used in a composition tells us something and generates specific responses. In this respect, consider the difference between an advertisement for groceries, as found in any newspaper, and an advertisement for an expensive product, as found in any upscale magazine (Figures 3.8 and 3.9). Notice how there is no white or empty space in the supermarket ad, which is crammed with lists of items and their prices. In the

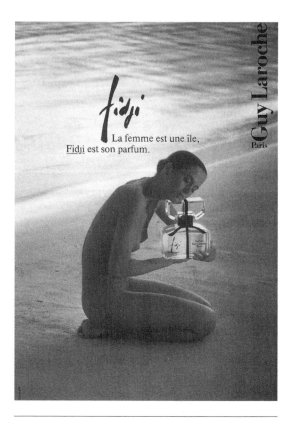

■ Figure 3.8

Detail from a supermarket advertisement. The supermarket advertisement attempts to convey as much information about as many products as it can and thus tends to be crowded with lists.

■ Figure 3.9

Advertisement for Fidji perfume. Advertisements for upscale products tend to be simple.

upscale product advertisement, on the other hand, there is a great deal of white space.

Our attitudes or feelings about what space means are quite likely based on associations and are metonymic. White space becomes associated with upper-class or upscale products and lifestyles, and so we learn to "read" the use of white space in a certain way. This reading is a coding we learn; as we grow up, we learn many codes that help us make sense of the advertisements and other visual phenomena to which we are exposed.

Balance

There are essentially two kinds of *balance*: axial and asymmetrical. With *axial,* or *formal,* balance, the elements of the composition are arranged equally on both sides of imaginary axes in the composition. This design is very formal and static. With *asymmetrical,* or *informal,* balance, the situation is different;

there is no desire to have balance—in fact, imbalance is deliberate, and the asymmetry generates stress, energy, and visual excitement.

We generally use the term *composition* to describe the way line, shape, volume, scale, and balance are used in a visual work, whether it be a painting or photograph or advertisement. Just as there are certain rules for writing words in the correct manner (what we call grammar and syntax), there are also rules for assembling elements in a visual work.

Figures 3.9 and 3.10 demonstrate the two approaches to balance. In Figure 3.10, notice how formal and static the advertisement with the axial balance is, how it lacks dynamics, or movement. We associate this kind of balance with antiquity, formality, sophistication, and elegance; products that desire to generate this kind of impression often use axial balance. By contrast, the Fidji advertisement in Figure 3.9 uses asymmetrical balance to suggest dynamic movement. Products that wish to convey this feeling (and this includes most products) don't, as a rule, use axial balance. If you examine the two advertisements, you will notice that they convey different impressions, in part through their use of balance.

▌ FIGURE 3.10
Advertisement for See's Candies. This advertisement is very formal and uses axial balance to suggest restraint and quality. It has very little text and is organized in a symmetrical manner around imaginary vertical and horizontal axes.

Direction

Lines and shapes direct our eyes to move in certain directions. When we look at an image, our eyes tend to start in the upper left corner and then move around the image as we are directed by lines, shapes, and other phenomena.

Herbert Zettl uses the term *vector* for *direction* and shows how powerful vectors are in all the visual media. He defines a vector as a "force with a direction and a magnitude" (1973:386) and suggests that we must use the notion of vector fields in order to understand film and television, which present us with moving images.

In advertising, direction is often used to focus attention on certain kinds of information (textual, pictorial) that is of central importance. Our eyes are "led" to the copy and then to an image. An advertisement may exist in two dimensions and be just a moment in time; but by using vectors for directing our eyes, it is possible to give a kind of life to the advertisement, as we move throughout it. We look at different parts of it and read all kinds of different meanings into it. We do the same for paintings and photographs and most other visual phenomena.

Lighting

The kind of light we find in an image is extremely important. Our ability to see anything is a function of light; at night, as the saying goes, all cats are gray. Light can be used to direct the eyes.

And lighting shapes our perceptions of things—it shows us what things look like by illuminating shape, texture, and color and by manipulating shadows to generate certain feelings and attitudes. Lighting is one of the tools that artists and photographers can control and is an extremely powerful aesthetic device.

There are two basic kinds of lighting: *flat lighting,* in which the differences between light and shadow are more or less minimized, and *chiaroscuro* (kee-are-oh-skoo-ro) lighting, in which the differences between light and shadow are emphasized (Figures 3.11 and 3.12). Flat lighting reaches its extreme in hospital operating rooms, where shadows are, to the extent it is possible, eliminated. Chiaroscuro (in Italian, its two parts mean "clear" and "obscure"), with its strong lights and shadows, is associated with works of intense emotion—photographs of the dead and horror films, for instance. The list on the following page gives the basic differences between chiaroscuro and flat lighting.

▌ FIGURE 3.11
Chiaroscuro lighting. This photograph has very strong lights and darks, giving it a dramatic quality.

▌ FIGURE 3.12
Flat lighting. This photograph reveals more than the one with chiaroscuro lighting but has less impact.

Flat	*Chiaroscuro*
Strong light, weak shadows	Strong lights and shadows
Rationality, knowledge	Emotion very powerful
Soap opera	Tragedy, horror film
Operating room	Graveyard

Naturally, lighting exists in all degrees of strength or intensity, depending on the purpose being served, and a given kind of lighting can be used in many different ways.

The French semiotician Roland Barthes recognized the power of lighting. In *Mythologies* (1957:15), he discussed professional wrestling and suggested, in his chapter on "The World of Wrestling," that

> the virtue of all-in wrestling is that it is the spectacle of excess. Here we find a grandiloquence which must have been that of ancient theatres. And in fact wrestling is an open-air spectacle, for what makes the circus or the arena what they are is not the sky . . . it is the drenching and vertical quality of the flood of light.

Even hidden in the most squalid Parisian halls, wrestling partakes of the nature of the great solar spectacles, Greek drama and bullfights: in both, a light without shadow generates an emotion without reserve.

What Barthes points out is that *it is the nature of the lighting that establishes, in essence, the intensity of the experience for people.* Other examples might be our association of a kind of lighting with the holy; think of cathedrals and their shafts of light.

Shadows help us gain orientation by defining space, by offering information about its contours. Shadows, which are generated by a light source falling on an object, reveal a good deal about the shape and location of objects. There are two kinds of shadows: *attached* shadows, which are on an object, and *cast* shadows, which are cast on some surface by the object. Cast shadows often reveal the shape of an object, though they can generate distortions as well.

Lighting, then, plays an important role in visual communication by directing our attention to certain things and intensifying our experiences. The fact that lighting "makes us" see and feel in a certain way must not be underestimated; it has a coercive element to it, like many other aspects of visual communication.

Lighting also can be therapeutic, and lighting therapy is often prescribed for people who suffer from midwinter depression. By exposure to simulated summer lighting conditions, relative to the time the sun rises and the amount of light people experience during a given day, these sufferers can experience relief from their symptoms.

Perspective

As strange as it might seem, what we call *linear perspective* is a relatively recent development in the arts; the ancient and early medieval painters did not know how to create the illusion of depth or of three dimensions on a two-dimensional plane, which explains why their work seems so flat— though it is often quite beautiful. Perspective was, one might say, "discovered" during the Renaissance (Figures 3.13). *Perspective* involves representing things the way they look, with parallel lines converging on some point (imaginary or real) on the horizon line via the process of psychological closure.

Psychological closure refers to the way our minds "complete" incomplete visual material that is given to us (Figure 3.14). We fill in the blanks, so to speak. We also form a *gestalt* or "whole" out of bits and pieces of information that we have—unifying them into something that is more than the sum of

This drawing, created during the Renaissance, shows that artists during this period had become masters of perspective.

█ FIGURE 3.14
This drawing leaves a great deal of information out, forcing viewers to rely on their eyes and previous experiences to achieve "psychological closure."

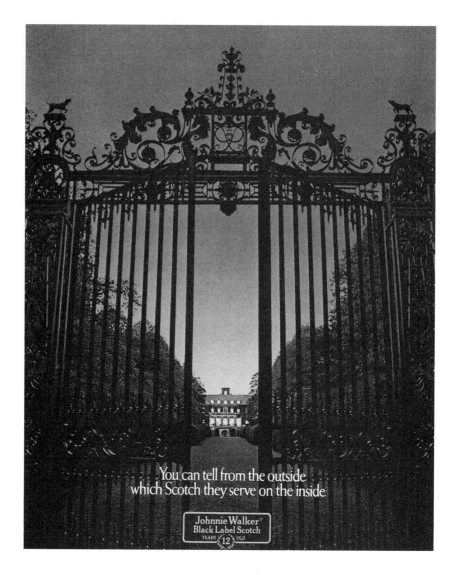

the parts. This process works every time we watch television, as Zettl explains (1973:137):

> The low-density (possessing relatively small amount of visual information due to
> the limited number of scanning lines) television picture relies quite heavily on
> our facility for psychological closure. Although our persistence of vision ("see-
> ing" something for a short period after it has already been removed from our
> vision) helps us to perceive the scanning dot of the TV image as a complete
> image, we need to apply psychological closure to relate the low-information pat-
> terns on the screen into meaningful visual images.

This process, which also is at work when we look at photographs with halftones (variations in shades of gray), is automatic and not dependent on our wills or intentions.

Look at Figure 3.15. Notice how the lawn and the sky (given direction by the trees) converge on the horizon line, where we find the mansion. This is an excellent example of one-point perspective, in which our eyes are led to one point (the vanishing point) that exists on the horizon line. (There is also two-point perspective, in which we sometimes don't see the second point but can infer or imagine it from looking at the work.) This vanishing point is the focal point of Figure 3.15, and just under it, highlighted by color, we find a message in white and a Johnnie Walker sign in yellow. These two elements are outside the massive gate, which signifies power, through its size, and taste, through its delicate and beautiful ironwork.

Now examine a work that does not make use of perspective, Angelo Puccinelli's *Tobit Blessing His Son,* the work of a fourteenth-century Italian painter (Figure 3.16). Unlike modern paintings, in this painting objects dis-

▌ FIGURE 3.16
Angelo Puccinelli, *Tobit Blessing His Son,* circa 1350–1399. This work, created before perspective had been discovered, reflects a different way of rendering reality.

tant from us are not reduced in size. This does not mean that works created before the mastery of perspective are inferior; many of these works are exquisite, but they are products of a different aesthetic system.

The placement of a horizon line generates a certain sense of spatiality (or lack of it) that has emotional consequences. The horizon line we see in the far western United States, which stretches out before us endlessly, suggests for most people an immensity and grandeur that we feel is somehow ennobling. Not being able to discern a horizon line often has the opposite effect; it can make us feel trapped and uneasy.

Proportion

Proportion involves the relationships of elements in an image or some other visual phenomenon. One of the most famous "laws" of proportion is that of Pythagoras, who is supposed to have discovered "the golden section." This law states that in a line, for example, the relationship of a small segment to a large segment should be the same as the relationship of the large segment to the entire line:

$$\text{L}_____|\_\_\_\_\_\text{J}$$
$$\text{X} \qquad\qquad \text{Y} \quad \text{Z}$$

YZ is to XY as XY is to XZ.

This relationship is found all through visual phenomena—in paintings, in architecture, in advertisements—because the eye finds it naturally pleasing.

When you deal with proportion, the following factors should be considered:

Size	Large	Small
Shape	Regular	Irregular
Axis	Vertical	Horizontal
Color	Light	Dark
	Warm	Cold
	Bright	Dull

All of these factors play a role in the way we create and respond to visual images.

COLOR

Color is, it turns out, a rather complex and bewildering phenomenon. Studies by psychologists have revealed that color affects our emotions and feelings and can be used to shape people's behavior. Thus, hospitals paint the walls

CHECKLIST FOR ANALYZING PRINT ADVERTISEMENTS

There is a distinction between commercials, which are broadcast on television, radio, and other electronic media, and advertisements, which are found in the various print media, such as magazines, newspapers, billboards, and posters. (On the Internet, the many static advertisements are, I would suggest, best seen as electronically disseminated print advertisements.) The following checklist focuses on print advertisements; Chapter 6 provides a checklist for analyzing television commercials.

The Mood

1. What is the general ambience of the advertisement—the mood that is created, the feelings it stimulates?

The Design

2. What is the basic design of the advertisement? Does it use axial balance, or are the fundamental units arranged in an asymmetrical manner?

3. What relationship exists between the pictorial aspects of the advertisement and the copy, or written material?

4. How is spatiality used in the advertisement? Is there lots of white (blank) space, or is the advertisement crowded —full of written and graphic material?

5. Is there a photograph used in the advertisement? If so, what kind of shot is it? What angle is it taken from? What is the lighting like? How is color used?

The Context and Content

6. If there are figures in the advertisement (people, animals), what are they like? Consider factors (to the extent that you can) such as facial expressions, hairstyles and hair color, body shape and body language, clothes, age, sex, race, ethnicity, education, occupation, relationships, and so on.

7. What does the background of the figures suggest? Where is the action taking place, and how does the background relate to this action?

8. What is going on in the advertisement, and what significance does this action have? Assuming that the advertisement represents part of a narrative, what can we conclude about what has led to this particular moment in time? That is, what is the plot?

Signs and Symbols

9. What symbols and signs appear in the advertisement? What role do they play in stimulating positive feelings about or desire for the product or service being advertised?

Language and Typefaces

10. How is language used in the advertisement? What linguistic devices provide information or generate some hoped-for emotional response? Does the advertisement use metaphor? Metonomy? Repetition? Alliteration? Comparison and contrast? Sexual innuendo? Definitions?

11. What typefaces are used, and what messages do these typefaces convey?

Themes

12. What are the basic themes in the advertisement? What is the advertisement about? (For example, the plot may involve a man and a woman drinking, and the theme may be jealousy.)

13. What product or service is being advertised? What role does it play in American society and culture?

14. What political, economic, social, and cultural attitudes are reflected in the advertisement—such as alienation, sexism, conformity, anxiety, stereotyped thinking, generational conflict, obsession, elitism, loneliness, and so on?

15. What information do you need to make sense of the advertisement? Does it allude to certain beliefs? Is it a reflection of a certain lifestyle? Does it assume information and knowledge on the part of the person looking at the advertisement?

of certain rooms peach and other warm and "friendly" hues to soothe and relax people. One color researcher, Faber Birren, suggests that different personality types tend to like particular colors—active people like red, friendly people like orange, high-minded people like yellow, and fastidious people like blue-green. Birren also suggests that introverted Nordic people tend to like cool colors, like greens and blues, while extraverted Latinos tend to like warm colors, like reds and oranges.

The color black is generally associated with death in the United States. Thus, it makes sense to avoid black in hospitals and foods. Recently, soft drink companies have marketed clear sodas to suggest purity. And white, which used to stand for goodness in bread, now stands for lack of quality (and perhaps an element of sterility) and has been supplanted by darker hues, which are associated with healthfulness and naturalness.

Philosophical Speculations on Color

In his book *An Enquiry Concerning Human Understanding,* published in 1777, the great philosopher David Hume speculated about color. Hume is famous for attacking the notion of cause and effect, arguing that we never see "necessary" connections between things that happen one after another. In his book, Hume suggested that ideas ultimately result from our sense impressions—what we hear or see or feel. According to Hume (1777:17), "All our ideas or more feeble perceptions are copies of our impressions or more lively ones."

This observation led Hume to speculate on color (1777:19):

> I believe it will readily be allowed that the several distinct ideas of colour, which enter by the eye, or those of sound, which are conveyed by the ear, are really different from each other; though, at the same time, resembling. Now if this be true of different colours, it must be no less so of different shades of the same colour; and each shade produces a distinct idea, independent of the rest. For if this should be denied, it is possible, by the continual gradation of shades, to run a colour insensibly into what is most remote from it; and if you will not allow any of the means to be different, you cannot, without absurdity, deny the extremes to be the same.

Hume is arguing that not only colors but shades of a particular color differ from one another. And this *must* be the case, Hume added. If it weren't, a person showing you different shades of a given color could ultimately force you to admit that quite a different color is a shade of the original color. This explains why the human eye is capable of distinguishing between an incredible number of colors and shades of colors.

The Enigma of Color

Color is an enigma. It is generated by electromagnetic waves; various wavelengths or combinations of wavelengths reflected off an object send messages to our eyes. Our eyes then interpret these wavelenghs as a given color or combination of colors. If you pass a beam of sunlight through a glass prism, you will see a series of colors, called rainbow or spectral colors, that fall within the visible electromagnetic spectrum, which is between 400 and 700 nanometers.

Each color has a different wavelength and thus travels through the glass prism at a different speed: red has the longest wavelength and travels through the prism faster than blue does. The sequence is always the same: red, orange, yellow, green, blue, indigo, violet.

When we see an object that reflects back most of the light falling on it, we see it as white. When we see an object that absorbs most of the light falling on it, we see it as black. (Neither black nor white are true colors; along with gray, they are neutral or achromatic—that is, without hue or chroma.) But the process of "seeing" colors is more complicated than it seems. As Jeremy Wolfe writes in *The Mind's Eye* (1986:vii,viii):

> The first step of visual processing is to get external stimuli into the nervous system. We see "light," a narrow band of energy from the electromagnetic spectrum. At the back of the eye lies the retina, a collection of nerve cells that is, in fact, an extension of the brain. The optics of the eye form an upside-down image on the retina, and photosensitive cells convert electromagnetic energy into the electrochemical signals that are understood by the nervous system. . . . The receptors in the retina give the nervous system a point-by-point assessment of the intensity of light. This input, further processed by other nerve cells in the retina, then moves down the optic nerve and into the brain. After an intermediate stop it arrives at the visual cortex, where we find cells that extract specific features of visual input. Where are there edges? What is moving? What is the size of the spot? What is the color? . . . The visual system has special mechanisms to extract information about features such as color, motion, orientation, and size. It is this information that "the mind's eye" uses to create visual perception.

Wolfe points out that he uses the term *create* deliberately, because what we see is based, it turns out, on inferences the mind makes about the world—which are based on mental input and on perceptual rules.

All of this takes place very quickly and appears to be automatic, but because seeing is based on inferences by the brain, it isn't as simple as it seems. In addition, as *The Mind's Eye* points out, other species (fish, snakes, insects) also see the world, but the world they see is quite different from ours—due, among other things, to differing eye structures.

Attributes of Color

There are a number of attributes of color that we might consider, including the following.

HUE. Hue refers to the colors themselves (and, indirectly, their location in the color spectrum or in a color wheel). The primary hues are red, yellow, and blue, and mixing any two of them gives the secondary colors:

Red + yellow = orange

Yellow + blue = green

Red + blue = violet

Most of the colors we see are not pure hues, but combinations of several wavelengths. Color theorists often use a "hue wheel" to show colors in their rainbow order—with red at the top and blue at the bottom. This hue wheel or color wheel is made by alternating the primary and secondary colors (that is, juxtaposing the primary and secondary color triads) and adding some intermediate colors. Colors that fall opposite one another on the wheel are known as complementary colors. When these complementary colors are mixed together, they produce gray.

SATURATION. Saturation refers to the strength, intensity, or purity of a color. Saturation is a function of the degree to which a color is not adulterated by having white or black mixed into it. (The Greek term *chroma* means "color" and is sometimes substituted for saturation.) White, gray, and black have no chroma or color saturation, and so are achromatic.

BRIGHTNESS. Brightness involves luminance—the lightness or darkness (or tonal gradations) of an image. Brightness is related not to color itself, but to the intensity of light generated by an object. Thus, a given screen image (a still) shown on a color television set and a black-and-white television set will have the same brightness. The brightness of a color is a function of the amount of light the color reflects.

WARMTH AND COOLNESS. We describe certain colors—red, orange, and yellow—as warm and other colors—blue and green—as cool. By mixing elements of cool colors into warm, we can cool down the warm colors, and by adding elements of warm colors into cool, we can warm them up.

CONTEXTUAL RELATIONSHIPS. Colors are affected by other colors near them. A given color can be made to seem weaker or stronger, depending on the colors that are placed next to it. If a circle of bright yellow is placed in a square of gray, for instance, the yellow will look different than it would if placed in a square of bright red. In the same way that concepts derive their meaning from the context in which they are found, colored shapes have an impact based on the context in which they are found.

In his 1971 book *Interaction of Color,* Joseph Albers, a painter and color theorist, focused on directly perceiving colors and examining their interactions. He showed, for example, that a square of gray placed on a green background appears pink and that a dark color appears light if placed on a background that is even darker. For instance, a square of light gray on a light gray background appears to be the same as a darker square of gray on a much darker background.

Albers also argued that figure and ground colors (such as a square of one color, a figure, placed in a larger square, its ground) affect each other simultaneously. In sum, with colors, as with words, as Saussure pointed out, relationships are of crucial importance.

CONCLUSIONS

Marshall McLuhan, the Canadian communications theorist, argued that "the medium is the message." He meant that a medium (such as television or radio) was more important than the content (the various programs, commercials, announcements, and so on) it carried. This position is obviously extreme, but McLuhan was correct in calling our attention to the power of the media—and, relative to our concerns, visual images—which many people tend to neglect.

As we can see from this primer in applied aesthetics, an image (such as those we see in a magazine advertisement or on our television screen) is an extremely complex phenomenon. Factors such as line, shape, dimension, lighting, design, spatiality, color, and perspective all can be looked at as conveying "messages" or being kinds of sign information that have an impact on us. Sometimes, we are aware of this impact; but sometimes, the message goes to our unconscious where, it can be argued, the message might have profound effects on us. (The "messages" we get from artists and writers often move from their unconscious to ours; they don't know the full extent of what they are doing, and we don't know the full extent of how we are being affected.) Anyone who has ever seen an advertisement for a product and experienced a strong desire to purchase it knows that visual phenomena are powerful motivators. Artists, writers, and other creative people can, as they say, "push our buttons" (Figure 3.17).

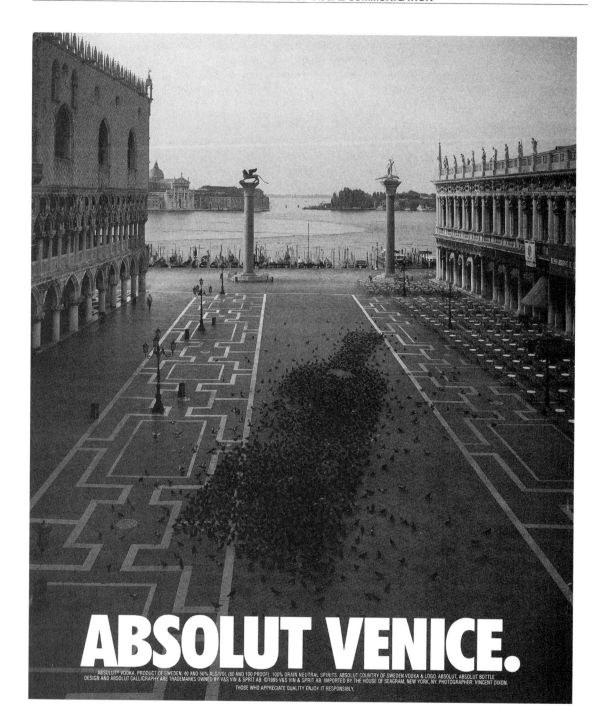

▮ FIGURE 3.17
This is one of a series of brilliant Absolut vodka ads that represent their distinctive bottle in various ways. Here pigeons in Venice form the bottle.

This chapter was written to illuminate some of the basic elements found in visual communication; knowing about these elements might help us understand the ways in which we can be stimulated and excited and have our buttons pushed. In the chapters to follow, you will see that these elements keep appearing and reappearing, for they are the building blocks from which all visual phenomena are constructed.

APPLICATIONS

1. Examine urban areas and malls to determine how scale is dealt with. How does scale shape our feelings in downtown "urban canyons"? How do huge malls and stores deal with scale?

2. Collect a number of images (photographs, advertisements, film stills, and the like) that have different kinds of spatiality. What generalizations can you make about spatiality and taste, class, and gender?

3. Examine lighting in different images. How do you think the lighting affects viewers? Do you notice different kinds of lighting used for different products in magazine advertisements? In different kinds of magazines?

4. When you watch television programs, focus your attention on the lighting. What generalizations can you make about the kinds of lighting used in different kinds of shows?

5. Do a research project on the psychological impact of perspective, and write a report. Why did it take so long for people to "discover" perspective? What kind of feelings do you get when you look at an early work of art that doesn't use modern perspective?

6. What do you think is the relationship between the medium and the message? What effects does a medium have on the messages it carries? Are there any cases in which a message is not affected, in significant ways, by the medium that carries it? If so, give some examples and explain why not. If you do believe that the medium affects the message, give some examples to justify your view.

7. What is your favorite color? Why? Do you think different personality types prefer different colors? If so, explain. Do you think there's a dif-

ference in the kinds of colors that people in warm and cold climates like? If so, explain.

8. Look at several packages in terms of the colors they use. What kinds of feeling do these colors generate in you? Why do you think the artists who designed these packages chose those particular colors? Redesign the package and change the colors. Explain what changes you made and why you made them.

9. Do a research project on the psychology of color, and write a report on your discoveries. What have psychologists discovered about how colors affect us? What did you learn about yourself from this investigation?

4

PHOTOGRAPHY:
The Captured Moment

Photography is interesting because it is both a popular and an elite art. It can function simply as a record of experiences (snapshots of people in front of tourist attractions), but it can also impose an artist's vision on what is being photographed (portraits by great photographers).

THE PHOTOGRAPH

Photography was invented in 1839 by Louis Jacques Daguerre and Joseph Niépce in France and, independently, by Henry Fox Talbot in England. The Daguerre method used sensitized metal (and could not be reproduced), while the Talbot method used a paper negative process that led, eventually, to modern photography as we now know it. The American George Eastman, who founded Eastman Kodak, made further refinements that led to roll film, which was introduced in 1881 and led, ultimately, to the modern motion picture.

Photography involves the following processes:

1. Using a camera to take a picture on light-sensitive film
2. Developing or processing this film and making a negative
3. Using this negative to make prints on light-sensitive paper

The result of this process is the photograph, the dominant form of permanent image in the modern world.

Human visual perception is a far more complex and selective process than that by which a film records. Nevertheless the camera lens and the eye both register images— because of their sensitivity to light—at great speed and in the face of an immediate event. What the camera does and what the eye can never do, is to *fix* the appearance of that event. It removes its appearance from the flow of appearances and it preserves it. . . . The camera saves a set of appearances from the otherwise inevitable supercession of further appearances. It holds them unchanging. And before the invention of the camera nothing could do this, except, in the mind's eye, the faculty of memory.

–JOHN BERGER,
ABOUT LOOKING

A *photograph* can be defined as an image, in the form of a positive print, taken by a camera (a device with a lens and shutter) and reproduced, permanently, on a photo-sensitive surface. Cameras range from the cheap throwaway models currently being produced to very expensive German and Japanese models with powerful lenses and many automatic features.

GENRES IN PHOTOGRAPHY

The term *genre*, French for "kind" or "type" or "category," is used to classify works in a given medium. We distinguish between a medium—such as print, radio, television, film, or photography—and the genres or kinds of works found in each medium. For example, television is a medium that includes (and also affects) genres such as soap operas, commercials, news shows, sports programs, talk shows, and so on. In the same light, photography is a medium that includes a number of different genres. Some of the most important genres of photographs are discussed here.

Art Photos

Works of fine art by gifted photographers who exploit the aesthetic elements of photography to their fullest (to create works that are considered "high" art) are now found in the photography collections of many museums. The great photographers traditionally worked in black and white—in part, because color photography had not been developed when some of them were doing their work. Even now, many art photographers prefer to work in black and white, though this is slowly changing. Also, new developments in digital cameras and image manipulation are having an impact on photography.

Snapshots

Photographs taken by ordinary people, typically showing their children growing up, sights seen in their travels, and special events, are a form of personal documentation (Figures 4.1 and 4.2). (Portraits can be art photographs, but more often, they are simply formal versions of the snapshot.) Because these snapshots are taken by amateurs, the persons being shot often are somewhat stiff, and the spatiality and other design elements in the picture are not very good. When people travel, they generally photograph them-

❙ FIGURE 4.1
A formal portrait of President Bill Clinton.

selves in front of "the sights" to document that they have been there and to remind themselves, when they look at their photos or slides later, of their experiences.

Photojournalism

In newspapers and magazines, photographs are used for their documentary and illustrative powers. These photographs show us the important events and people we read about and augment the information we get from the printed word. As Kevin G. Barnhurst points out in his 1994 book *Seeing the Newspaper,* there's a considerable amount of debate about the role of photojournalists. Some analysts focus on their role as chroniclers of reality, while others suggest there is an ideological content to their work—whose pictures they take, what angles they use, when the pictures are taken, and how they are used to "tell" a story.

❙ FIGURE 4.2
"Snapshot" of President Ronald Reagan. Informal portraits convey a considerably different impression of people than do formal ones, as the formal portrait of President Bill Clinton in Figure 4.1 demonstrates. Reagan is portrayed here in a natural setting, has powerful arms, is informally dressed, and has a larger-than-life quality about him. Technically, this photograph isn't really a snapshot, but rather an informal shot that gives the feeling of being a snapshot and may be seen as an example of Reagan's ability to give people "illusions" about himself.

Barnhurst (1994:43) discusses an exhibition of press photos held at The Museum of Modern Art in 1973 in which the curator, John Szarkowski, assigned certain "roles" to the photos:

> Seen as a whole, press pictures contain a kaleidoscope flow of particular faces within a few permanent roles. Szarkowski, with the aid of Diane Arbus, among others, selected the most "compelling" and "original" pictures, judged by their formal and iconographic contribution to the vocabulary of roles. The organization of the exhibit demonstrated a few of these roles: participants in a ceremony, the loser and the winner, victims of disaster, the bizarre, partakers in the good life, the contestant, the hero.

There is, then, a hidden structure to photojournalism—a set of roles that reveal themselves in the kinds of photographs that are taken. Presumably, these roles are the newsworthy ones in our society. Whether these roles are the most significant, as far as revealing what is going on in the social and the political realms, is another question.

Photodocumentaries

The photodocumentary is a visual form of sociology and anthropology meant to capture images of importance that social scientists and others can use to get a sense of what a group of people is like (Figures 4.3a and 4.3b). We now consider it important to have a record of how people live: their homes, their clothes, the objects they have in their homes, the foods they eat, the rituals they participate in, and so on. Scholarly journals published by visual anthropologists and visual sociologists are devoted to furthering the development of these disciplines. The camera is now an extremely important element of fieldwork for anthropologists and has revolutionized the way anthropologists work. (The same could be said for the Super 8 film camera and now the video camera.)

Commercial Photography

Photographs in advertisements, packaging, record covers, posters, and billboards probably represent the dominant use of photography in contemporary society. The average American is exposed to huge numbers of these photographs each day.

As the result of the power of the photograph to record reality, oil painting has changed, and artists no longer focus so directly on reality. It can be argued that the photograph indirectly led to such movements as abstract

■ **Figure 4.3a**
This image, from Antonioni's enigmatic film *Blow-Up* (1966), reflects the fact that images often contain more information than we imagine. *Blow-Up* is about a photographer, Thomas, who inadvertently takes a photograph of a murder while it is being committed. During the period in which he was making this film, Antonioni said, "I put reality itself into question."

■ **Figure 4.3b**
The sexual aspects of photography are captured in this image (also from *Blow Up*) of the main character, Thomas, photographing a fashion model.

expressionism and op art, genres concerned not with being realistic and imitating reality, but rather with expressing emotions and feelings through the use of color, design, and related techniques.

THE PROBLEM OF OBJECTIVITY

In an article entitled "The Elemental Fascination of Portrait Photography," the art historian Dore Ashton writes (1989:B60):

> There is a considerable body of literature verging on the philosophic concerning the photographic image. But I think it is worth pointing out that nothing serious has ever been written about photography that does not, in one way or another, concede that any photograph is only part of a truth. In the exceedingly interesting struggle to define just what photography is, most commentators have sooner or later come up against the problem of interpretation. They have discovered that the photograph, once thought to be the most faithful of representations of reality, is just as dependent on conventions of seeing and epochal conditioning as is the non-mechanical work of art.

Variables in Photography

A photographer must make many decisions when doing a portrait. These variables show how complicated photography is and why we no longer can view photographs as merely a record of reality.

1. *The viewpoint*. How close should the photographer be? How much background should be included in the shot? Where will the photograph be taken?
2. *Framing*. Will the composition be balanced or unbalanced? What composition elements will be included in the photograph?
3. *The angle*. Should the photograph be taken from above, from below, from the side, or from straight on?
4. *Lighting*. How will the subject be lighted? What light effects will be used? Should the lighting be flat or chiaroscuro?
5. *Focus*. How sharply will the photograph be focused? Should some elements of the photo be blurred or in soft focus?
6. *The pose*. What should the person being photographed be doing? Will any props be used? What facial expression should the subject adopt?

Consider the difference between the poses in Figures 4.4 and 4.5. The mug shot is designed for a practical purpose, but the portrait is meant to reflect something about the person being photographed. Consider also the

■ **FIGURE 4.4**
Mugshot No. 7213. The purpose of a mug shot is purely practical—to shoot what a person looks like as clearly as possible.

■ **FIGURE 4.5**
What is it about this film still of the famous film comedian Buster Keaton that is so intriguing? His striking, maybe even acrobatic, pose? His deadpan facial expression? His body language? Something else? This photo leads us to consider how it is that photographers are able to capture our attention and affect our emotions.

impact of an acrobatic and seemingly gravity defying pose such as Buster Keaton's in Figure 4.5.

Because there are so many variables in photography—in terms of camera angles, use of light and dark, texture, and focus—we must recognize that a picture is always an *interpretation* of reality, not reality itself. A dozen photographers taking pictures of the same scene would come up with a dozen different views of it. The photographs would be similar as far as the subject matter is concerned but different as far as the actual photographs are concerned. Photography, though it is a mechanical process, does not automatically reproduce reality.

Evidence and Glamorization

In a mug shot, photography is used to record a person's likeness in as simple and uncomplicated a manner as possible. In the portrait, photography is used to capture the essence of someone's personality and character—one might sometimes say to "glamorize" the person. These two poles—*evidence and glamorization*—are the extremes between which photography operates.

In Figure 4.6, a beautiful young woman (who happens to be a ballerina) is shown smiling and, from her pose, looking right at us. She is tousling her

❚ Figure 4.6
Portrait of Alaina
Albertson. Notice the
expressiveness of this
woman's smile, her allur-
ing pose, and the way her
gaze focuses on the
viewer.

hair, a nonverbal form of communication that has erotic implications. Her face is expressive and radiant, and the pupils of her eyes are slightly dilated (or enlarged), a sign generally held to be an unconscious indicator of sexual interest and excitement.

Desire can also be evoked by making allusion to certain scenes or stories or individuals that are part of our collective frame of reference and signify romance, love, and related matters: Cleopatra, Romeo and Juliet, Helen of Troy, Marilyn Monroe—the list is endless. As Tony Schwartz (1974:24–25) writes in *The Responsive Chord:*

> The critical task is to design our package of stimuli so that it resonates with information already stored with the individual and thereby induces the desired learning or behavioral effect. Resonance takes place when the stimuli put into our communication evoke meaning in a listener or viewer. That which we put into the communication has no meaning in itself. The meaning of our communication is what a listener or viewer gets out of his experience with the communicator's stimulus.

In other words, the photographs we see every day are stimuli that "activate" us by setting off the appropriate responsive chord. These photographs (and advertising in general) exploit what is already in our heads, the cultural lore we have stored up as a result of our education and experiences.

Connected with this desire is a latent dissatisfaction with ourselves the way we are, as well as our hopes for a better self in the future (when we have purchased whatever product or service is being advertised). And so we live our lives, suspended in a sense, between the mug shot of everyday reality and the portrait and the life of glamor and romance that it promises us.

The Pose: Figure and Ground

Some photographs are taken randomly, as a shot suggests itself in the course of a given day or experience. But others—in particular, the portrait—are posed. We all like to think that we can "read" personality or character just by looking at a person's face, as if that face recorded or stored up, in some magical way, that person's experiences. Although we may often be able to do this to a degree, in many cases poses are a representation not of character, but of personality. The term *personality* comes from the word *persona,* which means "mask." Our personalities are masks that we present to the world, and the photograph may be capturing this mask and not our "real" selves.

How do we read a photograph for personality or character? (Or should we ask, "How do we misread a photograph?") First, background helps define the person in a portrait. Lawyers are frequently portrayed in their libraries, with rows and rows of law books behind them, suggesting the knowledge (and with knowledge, power) that this person has. We find portraits of poor people in their shacks, with only the barest of furniture or possessions; this ground helps define the figures. So the ground helps define the figure, just as the figure helps define the ground. This background and the objects in it provide us with information that helps us gain an understanding of the person being portrayed.

Second, the person's appearance influences our interpretations. We all have notions about what having blonde hair or a weak chin or being gap-toothed or very thin or fat or short or tall signifies. "Conventional wisdom" tells us what facial features and body shapes mean, and we apply this "wisdom" (which, of course, is often wrong) to the people we see in portraits. Facial expression is another way of conveying information—through such things as a smile, a frown, a look of puzzlement, or stoic resignation. We all can empathize with others because we reveal different emotions via our facial expressions.

Third, body language helps us read photographs. We are now aware that a whole world of nonverbal communication exists and that we are always communicating, whether we say a word or not. Thus, body language generates messages that we all can interpret. In addition to facial expression and body language, people use various props (in the theatrical sense of the term) to generate impressions. Some of the most important props include the following:

1. *Hairstyle.* Crewcuts, punk, long hair, the "Ollie North" look—all convey information about a person. With women, long, straight hair conveys a different impression than does short, curly hair. And as time progresses and hairstyles become popular or fade, we read people via hairstyles, which suggest that someone is "with it" or "square."

2. *Eyeglasses.* The style of eyeglasses tells us about the taste or lifestyle of the person wearing them. Now that contact lenses are so popular, a person who chooses to wear eyeglasses might be trying to create a certain impression.

3. *Fashion.* We have learned in recent years that fashion provides information and that there are various ways one dresses for "power." Think of the difference between a dark, pin-striped three-piece suit and jeans and a T-shirt.

4. *Jewelry.* The kind of jewelry one wears is a means of impression management. What does it mean when men wear earrings? What if a woman wears many pairs of earrings? Think about class rings and wedding rings. Jewelry or its lack is an important prop.

5. *Makeup.* A woman with a great deal of makeup seems to be quite different from a woman with no makeup at all (the "natural" look). Long, polished nails convey a certain image—associated with glamor—in our minds.

6. *Briefcases, attaché cases, bags, and so on.* These objects also generate impressions and are used by people for the purpose of impression management.

When we look at a photograph of a person or a group of people, we must decipher a great deal of visual detail if we are to get the full meaning of the photograph (Figure 4.7). We use our faces, our bodies, our clothes, and objects to create certain impressions in other people. To read photographs correctly requires background information or what might be called "consumer cultural literacy." If you do not recognize, for example, that a briefcase has the logo of an expensive Italian fashion house, you've missed something its owner wanted to convey.

TECHNICAL ASPECTS OF THE PHOTOGRAPH

A number of different technical matters should be considered when taking a photograph. We'll start our discussion of these with the most important—focus.

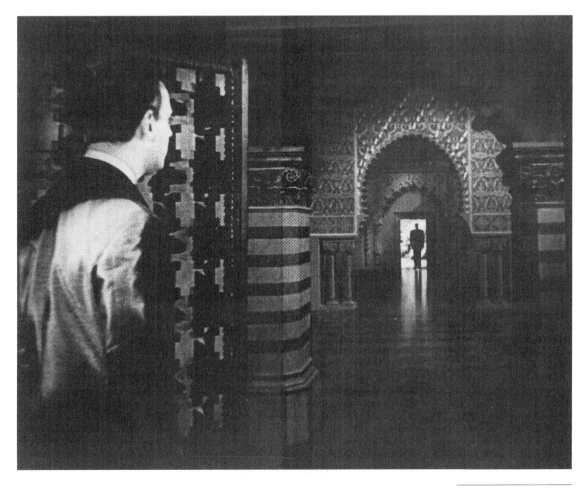

▌ FIGURE 4.7
This long shot from the film *Citizen Kane* achieves its dramatic quality by framing the figure in the door against a background of light. The image also is enhanced by the decorative nature and the huge size of the room.

Focus

Focus refers to the clarity of an image or part of an image. We use the term *depth of field* to refer to objects in focus in an image. This depth of field varies, depending on the kind of lens we use in the camera. We get greater depth of field with wide-angle lenses than with narrow-angle lenses. We can use focus to emphasize certain things and deemphasize others or to generate certain impressions. Thus, a soft focus is associated with the romantic and related emotional states and is often used in cosmetic advertisements, which sell magic and fantasy. By contrast, very sharp and clear focus is connected with science and pure rationality (Figures 4.8 and 4.9).

▌ FIGURE 4.8
Hard focus. Photo of Ludmila Lopukhova, formerly a principal dancer in the San Francisco Ballet.

▌ FIGURE 4.9
Soft focus. Photo of dancer Ludmila Lopukhova modified to achieve a more romantic look.

Grain

The term *grain* refers to the prominence of the minute dots that make up a photograph. Grainy photographs are associated with snapshots and photographs taken by chance or in difficult situations. Thus, we associate grain with realism and honesty. We do not use grainy photographs as a rule; and so when they are used, it suggests that something unusual has transpired or is being communicated.

Shot Angle

Angle refers to where the camera is relative to the subject of the photograph. A shot that "looks up" to the subject conveys a different impression (such as reverence?) than one that "looks down" on (and is superior to?) the subject. When we photograph people, the shot angle is quite important. A full-face shot conveys a different impression than does a three-quarter-face shot or a profile.

With the full-face shot, we find that the person being photographed is, in a sense, looking us directly in the eyes; and thus, this pose suggests honesty and candor. The three-quarter-face shot has been interpreted by Roland Barthes to suggest a person of vision, who is looking beyond us to the future. The person in the profile shot becomes an object of scrutiny, someone looked at. We find this angle in mug shots and in certain portraits, where a person's profile strikes the photographer as the best way to portray the subject.

Kinds of Shots

Here we are concerned with how far the camera is from the subject. The following list presents some of the most important shots, assuming that we are photographing a person, though we could be photographing an object or a building or a general landscape:

1. *The extreme close-up.* This might portray only part of a person's face.
2. *The close-up.* This generally would include the face but not much else of a person.
3. *The medium shot.* This would show the face and part of the torso.
4. *The long shot.* This would include the entire body and some of the surroundings.
5. *The extreme long shot.* Here the figure would be relatively small, with much of the surroundings shown. This shot functions as an establishing shot and suggests the context in which a given person or group of persons is to be found.

Each of these shots has a particular function and conveys a certain kind of message. The extreme close-up is very personal and intimate and is meant to give us insights into the personality of the person being photographed. As we move away from the camera in a perpendicular line (known as the *Z-axis*), we become less involved with personality and more involved with background or context. Close-up, medium, and long shots of a building are shown in Figures 4.10, 4.11, and 4.12.

Color

Photographers can use different kinds of coated lenses to manipulate color. They can deepen or emphasize certain colors and minimize others. Thus, color is one more variable that photographers can play with to create the effects they wish—such as making food in photographs look so mouthwateringly good.

❚ Figure 4.11
Medium shot of the White House. In this shot, we see the entire White House but nothing else.

❚ Figure 4.10
Close-up of the White House. Here we see just a portion of the White House.

❚ Figure 4.12
Long shot of the White House. Here we see the fountains in front of the White House and a bit of the environs. We are considerably farther away from the White House than we were in the medium shot.

Composition

When photographers print their negatives, they have an additional opportunity to manipulate images. They can create a composition that pleases them by selecting only a certain portion of the negative to use, a process known as *cropping*. A given negative can yield any number of different photographs, depending on the aesthetic interests of the photographer.

By playing with focus and depth of field, shot angles, kinds of shots, grain, color, and composition, photographers are able to create many different effects and generate many different meanings in a given situation (Figures 4.13 and 4.14). Photography is not a reflection or an imitation of reality, but an interpretation of reality. Therefore, seeing isn't always believing, because photographs only reveal, ultimately, what photographers want their photographs to reveal.

With developments in computer imaging, photographs can now be manipulated in remarkable ways, and changes made to them cannot be detected by the human eye. As a result, photographs no longer can be thought of as evidence, because with computers almost anything is possible. Again, seeing is not believing, and what you get is not always what someone saw.

As has been suggested earlier, what we see is, to a great degree, affected by what we know—the degree of cultural literacy we have and the extent to which we can understand allusions and references to things, can evaluate the socioeconomic significance of props and objects, and are in tune with the same codes as the photographer (or, in the case of advertisements, the copywriter and art director responsible for a given advertisement).

❙ FIGURE 4.13
Ansel Adams, *Leaves*. This is an example of an extreme close-up and shows that even simple objects often have aesthetic qualities.

(a)

❚ FIGURE 4.14
Two views of a Little League team. In (a), the subjects grouped themselves, and in (b), they were grouped by the photographer, yielding group portraits that differed a great deal.

(b)

ADVERTISING PHOTOGRAPHY AND OIL PAINTING

In *Ways of Seeing*, the English art critic John Berger points out that many of the devices found in advertising photography come from oil painting. He writes (1972:138):

> Compare the images of publicity [the English term for advertising] and paintings in this book, or take a picture magazine, or walk down a smart shopping street looking at the window displays, and then turn over the pages of an illustrated museum catalogue, and notice how similarly messages are conveyed by the two media. A systematic study needs to be made of this. Here we can do no more than indicate a few areas where the similarity of the devices and aims is particularly striking.

A partial list of the items mentioned by Berger (1972:138) follows. Notice the degree to which information *in the mind of the observer* is crucial to interpreting these images correctly:

The gestures of models (mannequins) and mythological figures.
The romantic use of nature (leaves, trees, water) to create a place where innocence can be refound.

The exotic and nostalgic attraction of the Mediterranean.

The poses taken up to denote stereotypes of women: serene mother (madonna), free-wheeling secretary (actress, king's mistress), perfect hostess (spectator-owner's wife), sex-object (Venus, nymph surprised), etc. [Figure 4.15]

The special sexual emphasis given to women's legs.

The materials particularly used to indicate luxury: engraved metal, furs, polished leather, etc.

The gestures and embraces of lovers, arranged frontally for the benefit of the spectator.

The physical stance of men conveying wealth and virility.

All of these images come from the world of oil painting, which had the mission (before the development of photography) of celebrating private

▌FIGURE 4.15
William Beckman, *Diana IV,* 1981. Which stereotype of women, as discussed by John Berger, applies to this painting?

property and suggesting, as Berger puts it, that "you are what you have" (see Figure 4.15). This task has now been taken over by photography and, through the institution of advertising (a $200-billion industry in America), is spread to the masses.

What advertising does, Berger suggests, is make us marginally dissatisfied with our lot so that we pin our hopes on a better future, obtainable through purchasing products and services that will enhance our sense of well-being. For the working classes, advertising promises (1972:145) "a personal transformation through the function of the product it is selling (Cinderella); middle-class publicity promises a transformation of relationships through a general atmosphere created by an ensemble of products (The Enchanted Palace)." These implied promises are tied to the power of the image to create desire as well as to generate a certain amount of anxiety, and the two are linked together. Wherever we find desire, we also find anxiety.

THE IMAGE AND CAPITALISM

We can push this analysis of the image and society up one rung on the ladder of abstraction by examining the ideas of Susan Sontag. She suggests in *On Photography* that capitalist societies need photographic images (1973: 178,179):

> A capitalist society requires a culture based on images. It needs to furnish vast amounts of entertainment in order to stimulate buying and anesthetize the injuries of class, race, and sex. And it needs to gather unlimited amounts of information, the better to exploit natural resources, increase productivity, keep order, make war, give jobs to bureaucrats. The camera's twin capacities, to subjectivize reality and to objectify it, ideally serve these needs and strengthen them. Cameras define reality in the two ways essential to the workings of an advanced industrial society: as a spectacle (for masses) and as an object of surveillance (for rulers). The production of images also furnishes a ruling ideology. Social change is replaced by a change in images. The freedom to consume a plurality of images and goods is equated with freedom itself. The narrowing of free political choice to free economic consumption requires the unlimited production and consumption of images.

From Sontag's perspective, the photographic image has rather ominous and sinister dimensions. Whether her analysis is correct is a matter for debate; but she does point out the power and usefulness of the photographic image and the complex role these images play in modern societies.

THE PHOTOGRAPH AND NARCISSISM

The photograph is used as a record of our existence and that of our loved ones. Thus, when we have young children, we take many pictures of them as they develop. We also take pictures of ourselves on trips as proof, so to speak, that we actually made the trip and as a way of indirectly indicating that we exist and are participating in history. This explains why we often take snapshots of our loved ones (or induce others to take pictures of us and our loved ones) in front of hotels, statues, palaces, churches, temples, and other sites of significance.

There is also an *autoerotic* element to the photographs we take of ourselves. If modern societies subject us to the stresses John Berger and Susan Sontag write about, there is some measure of consolation in retreating into ourselves, into what might be described as an imagistic form of narcissism. Like Narcissus, the mythological figure who fell in love with his own reflection, our photographs do have a powerful self-referential eroticism about them. We may not go as far as Narcissus, but we do have strong feelings about our image, as presented to us by photographs.

That might explain why we complain so often about photographs taken of us that they "don't look like" us, aren't flattering, or don't do justice to us. One reason for this stems from the difference between the idealized image of ourselves that we "see" in the mirror and the harsh reality of the photograph. It is, of course, possible to have a photograph that really doesn't look like oneself; this happens from time to time.

And some photographs are terribly unflattering, due to the lighting or camera angle and that kind of thing. But more often than not, it is not the photograph that lies to us, but we who lie to ourselves. Or we lie to others by using photographs of ourselves that were taken many years back. It is quite natural to wish to present ourselves to others in the best possible light, which—in the instance of a portrait—often means (ironically) the least possible light.

CONCLUSIONS

There is a paradoxical aspect to the photographic image. It promises us truth but all too often is used to subvert and distort the truth. Pictures may not lie, but liars (that is, those who manipulate the truth with their images) take pictures—so we find ourselves necessarily ambivalent about the images that photography brings us. As Kiku Adatto points out in *Picture Perfect: The Art and Artifice of Public Image Making* (1993:23):

Over a century and a half after its invention, the promise and the paradox of photography are with us still. From video cameras mounted on Air Force jets, we record smart bombs descending upon their targets in the Persian Gulf and watch a war on television. At the same time, suspicious of pose, we wonder whether, for all the satellite hookups and video wizardry, we are really witnessing the truth of the war.

The modern revolution in the technology of picture-making has extended the potential of the camera for authentic documentation, but also has created the potential for the image to subvert reality on an unprecedented scale. We have played out the paradox of the artifice of imagery to a degree unimaginable to those who called the camera the "pencil of nature." They aspired to the "perfect picture," and judged the image by its fit with the world. In our image-conscious culture, we have reversed the words. We seek moments or events that are "picture perfect," and judge the world for its fitness as an image.

We see this reversal Adatto writes about in the selection of photographs used in newspapers and magazines and, most particularly, in the stories covered by television news. It is now the images, more than anything else, that determine what stories will be carried ("If it bleeds, it leads").

It turns out that much of the film footage we saw of the "smart bombs" did not tell us the whole truth. In fact, according to a government study, they were no more effective than ordinary weapons—though they were enormously more expensive. We saw only the successes of these smart weapons, not their many failures.

The photograph is, then, an extremely enigmatic and complicated item. It has enormous power, which means that we must always consider the ethics involved in taking photographs and using them. We use the photographic image in numerous ways, and photographic images pervade our modern society—making it what it is and, some would say, giving us images of ourselves that shape our sense of identity and our sociopolitical order.

Certain people (often in what we describe as nonliterate cultures) believe that if you have an image of a person, you have some kind of occult power over that person. We may laugh at such "superstitions," but if we consider the power of the photographic image more closely, these notions may not be so wrong. In the beginning was the word; shortly after that came the image; and when we put the two together, all kinds of remarkable things started to happen.

APPLICATIONS

1. Do you consider photography to be a fine art? If so, why? If not, why not?

2. What do you think is the difference between a snapshot and a photograph?

3. If you have access to photographs taken of you when you were growing up, examine them. What might they tell you about yourself and your family?

4. People frequently claim that photographs taken of them don't really look like them. Do you think this is correct? If so, how do you explain it? If not, why not?

5. Why is it that photographs have the power to evoke strong emotional responses in people? How would you explain this?

6. It has been suggested that photographs are very useful documents for people who want to find out about a culture. How can we use photographs this way? What do we look for? Find some photographs that you think have cultural significance and analyze them. What do you find?

7. Do you think a photograph can capture the essence of a person or merely the image of a person? Explain your position and justify your answer.

8. To what degree does what we know and bring to a photograph affect the way we respond to and interpret the photograph? If you never heard of the Holocaust and were shown pictures of people in the concentration camps, would the pictures have the same impact? Explain your answer.

9. Pretend you are a tourist and take a series of photographs that a tourist would take in your hometown or some area near you. Now pretend you are a visual anthropologist and take another series of photographs that an anthropologist would take in the same place. What differences do you find in the two series of photographs?

10. Assume you are commissioned by a photography magazine to take some portraits of your friends. Take some portraits in which you pose your subjects and try to capture their personality and character. Then answer these questions: What problems did you confront in taking these photographs? How well were you able to capture the personality and character of your subjects?

11. Use your camera to document a typical day in your life. What does this exercise reveal about you and your everyday life? Assuming your classmates do this exercise, what do their photographs reveal about their lives? Did you discover anything about your life or the lives of your friends that was surprising? How did you make sure you weren't giving

a false impression of your everyday life? How did you decide on which photographs to take?

12. Choose some subject that interests you and that has interesting pictorial possibilities and do a photo-essay on it. What is it like to write about a topic that you have also photographed? Was your photo-essay shaped primarily by what you wanted to show or what you wanted to say? Explain your answer.

5

FILM:
The Moving Image

Movies are a very complicated—and in recent years, a very expensive—art form. With the development of computer animation, just about anything in the way of special effects can be done in a movie now. In the final analysis, however, movies tell stories. If a movie doesn't tell a good story and have characters that audiences find interesting, all the special effects in the world can't make people go see it.

MOTION PICTURES

Movies have had a curious history. In their earliest days, they were regarded as miraculous but rather primitive amusements. Later, they were seen as entertainments, but not as a serious or significant art form. Now, the motion picture is considered an extremely important art form. Many films are seen by scholars as great works of art, and many directors are treated as great creative artists (or, as the French put it, "auteurs"). So the motion picture has come a long way, from popular art form to elite art form. In recent years, with the development of semiotics, the motion picture has been studied not only in terms of what it reflects about society and what ideological messages it carries but also, and perhaps primarily, in terms of how meaning is generated by what might be described as the grammar of film—the various kinds of shots and editing techniques that directors use to give shape to their vision.

Like painting and sculpture, film employs line, texture, color, form, volume, and mass, as well as subtle interplays of light and shadow. Many of the rules of photographic composition followed in the motion picture are similar to those applied in painting and sculpture. Like the drama, film communicates visually through dramatic action, gesture, and expression, and verbally through dialogue. Like music and poetry, film utilizes subtle and complex rhythms, and like poetry, in particular, it communicates through images, metaphors and symbols. Like pantomime, film concentrates upon the moving image, and like the dance, that moving image has certain rhythmic qualities.

–JOSEPH M. BOGGS
THE ART OF
WATCHING FILMS

95

A motion picture can be defined as a succession of discrete frames, projected at a rate of twenty-four frames per second (normal speed) that offers the illusion of motion—because an afterimage lingers in the eye that connects all the images together.

There are several variations on the speed at which scenes are filmed. Scenes filmed at greater-than-normal speed (but projected at twenty-four frames per second) seem to move slowly; this is called slow motion. When the reverse happens, and scenes are filmed at slower-than-normal speed and projected at twenty-four frames per second, we have fast motion (sometimes called "speeded" motion). There is also a device known as the "freeze-frame," where one image is continued for a period of time, stopping motion. This powerful effect is often used as a transitional device.

The basic unit of film is the *frame,* which is a discrete image. (Unlike film, television does not have frames.) The existence of discrete frames (or *stills*) makes it possible for film scholars to examine films in considerable detail and to reproduce certain frames of significance (Figure 5.1). Frames contain

▌ Figure 5.1
F. W. Murnau, detail of a frame from *Nosferatu,* 1922. Notice how this shot conveys horror. We look up at the vampire figure; he has sunken eyes, a deathlike expression on his face, and long, hideously curved fingernails.

an enormous amount of material—they are really analogous to the photographic images discussed in Chapter 4. But the complete motion picture involves combinations of frames and is based on what might be called *shots* (to be discussed shortly).

Films are not shot in sequence; different scenes are shot in different order, but all are merged into the proper sequence at the end of shooting—a process known as *editing* (Figure 5.2). Editing involves deciding how to arrange the segments of the film as a means of shaping the emotional responses of the viewers. A given amount of film footage, from the original shoots, can be shaped in many different ways, depending on the aesthetic sensibilities of the film editor.

In one sense, a film can be regarded as a work designed to generate certain desired emotional responses in viewers. This is somewhat of an oversimplification, but it points out the fact that filmmakers seek various effects; in fact, they often start with a given desired effect and work backwards, trying to figure out how to achieve the effect.

CONVENTIONS OF FILM EDITING

There are certain conventions or codes of editing that we all learn by experience, from watching numerous motion pictures. These conventions include the following:

1. *The wipe.* A new image replaces a previous one by a defined horizontal, vertical, or diagonal line that "wipes" the old image off the screen. This creates a sharp break with past action.
2. *The dissolve.* One image gradually fades or "dissolves" into a new image. This less radical break with past action often is used to suggest the passage of a good deal of time.
3. *The fade-out* or *fade-in.* The image gradually fades away to black (an empty screen) or fades in from an empty screen. Often, fade-outs and fade-ins are combined, but this need not be done.
4. *The flip-frame.* The frame appears to flip over into a new scene.
5. *The cut.* A sequence is stopped, and a complete new image is shown. When a number of cuts are used, to suggest a number of things going on at the same time (simultaneity) and excitement, it is called quick cutting.
6. *The defocus shot.* A scene ends by moving out of focus and a new scene begins out of focus and moves into clear focus. This device links the two scenes in the viewer's mind.

■ **Figure 5.2**
Sergei Eisenstein, *The Battleship Potemkin*, 1925. These frames, taken from the great Russian film, show how directors edit films—they vary the shots to provide information and to shape the emotional responses of viewers.

All of these devices are analogous to punctuation in writing; they are the means by which the director indicates (though not overtly) to viewers how they should relate scenes to one another. Someone unfamiliar with these editing conventions, is likely to misinterpret the film. As we grow up and watch films, we all learn, through trial and error, what the conventions are and how to respond to them.

SHOTS AND SHOT RELATIONSHIPS

We have already discussed shots in the chapter on photography. Because of the nature of film, however, some additional topics need to be dealt with here.

The Zoom Shot

Film makes possible the *zoom shot,* in which we use a lens to move in, smoothly, closer and closer on a subject, from a long shot or medium shot, until we arrive at a close-up (Figure 5.3). The zoom shot has the effect of intensifying an image, of making it possible to inspect an object or a person's face more closely. It is a message from the director that we must pay special attention to something and look for something that will be revealed to us. There is a suggestion of intimacy. Inexperienced directors sometimes become "zoom crazy" and use the zoom so often that it loses its novelty and impact.

In the same way, a reverse zoom, in which the lens moves away from a close-up of an object or a person, conveys the opposite emotion. Here we are being asked to take a larger view, to look at the big picture. Thus, this shot is

▌ FIGURE 5.3
Representation of a zoom shot sequence, in which we move from a long shot to a medium shot to a close-up.

meant to give us a picture of relationships and the overall structure of a situation. It suggests reason and distancing, not emotional involvement.

The Reaction Shot

Here the camera focuses on the reaction of a character to something said (the dialogue) or an event in the film. The *reaction shot* reveals, visually, how an important figure in the story has responded to something. This shot is meant to shape our perception of and emotional response to the dialogue or events that have just transpired.

Montage

This concept was developed by the film theorist and director Sergei Eisenstein, who used it in a number of different ways. In essence, Eisenstein argued in *Film Form* (1949:49), *montage* "is an idea that arises from the collision of independent shots—shots even opposite to one another . . ." Thus, we derive meaning in film from seeing shots in combination. One shot is, for all practical purposes, a photograph; but when shots are *combined* in certain sequences, we are led to have certain ideas or emotional responses. This explains, in part, the power of MTV, which often is exciting and experimental in its use of shots and editing.

Montage can involve such visual matters as graphic elements, planes, volumes, spatiality, and images of motion. By playing off one shot (or aspects of that shot) against another, we produce the meaning or effect that Eisenstein considers to be the basis of montage and, ultimately, of film (Figure 5.4). This calls to mind the notion of the Swiss linguist Ferdinand de Saussure, who argued in his *Course in General Linguistics* (1966:117) that "concepts are purely differential and defined not by their positive content but negatively by their relations with the other terms of the system." An image by itself can be made to mean anything, and it is only when we see this image or shot placed in relationship to another image or shot that we get a specific emotion or idea.

▌ **FIGURE 5.4**
Sergei Eisenstein, frame from The Battleship Potemkin, 1925. This image is one of his most famous. It shows a woman after she has been shot, with her blood spurting out. This and other images from this great film conveyed Eisenstein's sense of the horror of life under the czar.

COLOR IN FILM

Originally, films were black and white. When color film was introduced, it was something of a novelty, and seeing a color film was a special occasion. Films would advertise, for example, that they were in technicolor; and color films, because they were unusual, had a distinctive appeal and quality. Now, with few exceptions, all films are made in color. This means that black-and-white films now are unusual and signify that a film is a documentary or an "art" film or was made many years ago.

From our discussion in Chapter 3, we realize that color can generate powerful emotional responses, especially when combined with other elements of film. So color (or, in some cases, the lack of color) is one more tool used to enhance and intensify our responses to images.

Because of the arbitrary relationship that exists between a signifier (such as the use of color) and what is signified (such as madness), we should not automatically assume, however, that black and white is a preferred medium for showing the "darker" elements of the psyche. It has been pointed out, for example, that the extremely rich coloration of the film *Blue Velvet* signified emotional disorientation and pathology equally as well as did the use of shadows and distorted images in black-and-white films from earlier times.

SOUND

The first films did not have sound and relied on the images and captions or printed words to carry the narrative. The coming of sound, with *The Jazz Singer* in 1927, changed film dramatically, for now it was possible to use dialogue, sound effects, and music to shape the viewers' responses.

Spoken Dialogue

The conversation that characters carry on in a film is dialogue. Dialogue generally is tied to scenes, not to frames (which are single images). When the scene—which is a segment of a story with certain characters in a particular place—changes, so does the dialogue.

The dialogue tells us what people are doing and often, by inference, what they are thinking. Thus, dialogue helps the visual images carry the story along. Without sound, we can still get a pretty good idea of what is happening in a film, but our understanding is crude and simplistic. Often, a pattern of shots and countershots or reaction shots (or reverse-angle shots) matches the pattern of conversation in a scene. Using these conventions, directors let us know what the different characters are thinking (or seem to be thinking) and how they are responding to the conversation. It should be noted that film dialogue, like most conversation, is characterized by sentence fragments, interruptions, and overlapping speech. We do not, as a rule, always wait for others to stop speaking or speak in complete and beautifully structured sentences. And the dialogue generally is used to add something to the visual image, not to repeat the information the visual image offers us; the dialogue should add to the narrative but not replace the image.

We also must recognize that the language used in dialogue and the quality of a character's voice tell us a great deal. The human voice has an intrinsic capacity to generate emotions and thus adds to the power of the image—which explains why the motion picture is such a powerful medium.

Narration

In some films, such as documentaries, we find narration, in which a speaker (or several speakers) off the screen provides us with information relevant to the images we are seeing. Often, we have both narration and dialogue, as a narrator sets a scene for us and then the characters involved act out the scene. Sometimes, the narrator is also part of the action and steps in and out of the film to offer his or her comments. The narrator, as someone who is distanced from the action (even if only momentarily), can tell us things, offer opinions, and act as a kind of omniscient presence.

Narrators fill in gaps in a film's story line, provide important background information, tell us what we should think about various characters (and often what various characters are thinking), frame plots, and provide a tone to a film. As such, they are very useful in all kinds of films—whether they be dramatic films or documentaries or mixtures such as docudramas. The presence of a narrator suggests that a story or film is realistic and that it has documentary elements in it.

Sound Effects

Sound effects, which imitate the sounds associated with given phenomena, make a film seem realistic and natural. They also function as cues that shape our emotional responses. Thus, for example, a film about space might augment a scene of a rocket blasting off with the awesome power of an associated series of sounds. In the same vein, if the sound we hear does not correspond to our expectations and does not "go" with the event, we are immediately aroused and made suspicious.

There is some question about whether specific sounds always have a predictable effect on people. Semiotics would suggest that this is *not* the case: a given sound—such as a shriek—can be used, depending on the situation, to suggest joy and happiness or dread and terror. Recall that Saussure explained that a sign (which he defined as a sound or object) was arbitrarily or conventionally related to a given signifier or meaning. So any sound can be made to mean anything.

In *How to Read a Film,* James Monaco (1977:180,181) cites a French film theorist, Christian Metz, on the "five channels of information in a film: (1) the visual image; (2) print and other graphics; (3) speech; (4) music; (5) noise (sound effects). Interestingly, the majority of these channels are auditory rather than visual." And, he continues, there are only two continuous channels in this list—the visual image and noise/sound effects.

Sound in film is all-pervasive and helps create locales (room sound) and a sense of time. And, as we have developed technology with stereo, Dolby systems, and the like, the power of sound in film has been augmented.

Music

The music heard in the background of films plays a very important role, and many producers argue that the music in a film can mean the difference between a hit and a flop. Music is used to key the responses of viewers to particular scenes. This is done through the use of *motifs*—passages that become linked to certain kinds of events.

What generally happens is that we are taught to associate certain musical motifs with certain events or kinds of events. These motifs then can be used to trigger certain responses in us—we are, so to speak, conditioned and we respond accordingly (the same way Pavlov's dogs were taught to associate a bell with being fed and thus were conditioned to salivate when they heard the bell). Music has the power to speak directly to our emotions, so it helps intensify and dramatize scenes and augments the visual images. A good example of this is found in Philip Glass's synthesized musical score for the postmodern film *Koyaanisqatsi* (Figure 5.5).

As with sound effects, in almost all cases it is the association that is crucial, not some intrinsic quality in the music itself that automatically generates a specific emotional response in everyone who hears it.

SPECIAL VISUAL EFFECTS

A number of things can be done to affect the visual image, from simulated events (what we commonly describe as special effects) to holding the camera by hand and getting a certain look. In some cases, we keep the camera stationary and move the camera head or use a zoom lens; in other cases, we move the camera and its support in various ways.

▌ **FIGURE 5.5**
This is a scene from
Koyaanisqatsi, a post-
modern film made by
Godfrey Reggio in 1983.

▌ **FIGURE 5.5**
This is a scene from
Koyaanisqatsi, a post-
modern film made by
Godfrey Reggio in 1983.

The Hand-Held Camera

When a camera operator holds a camera and shoots with it, there is an unsteady, jerky quality to the resultant image suggesting that this is the kind of film we might get from a spectator at a scene who just happened to have a camera on hand. The lack of precision or absolute clarity engenders a sense of realism and truthfulness. So directors often use hand-held cameras when they want to counter the kind of image they get from using mounted cameras.

Camera Movement

A *pan* involves a camera head traveling horizontally across a person, object, or scene, while a *tilt* involves a camera head traveling vertically across a person, object, or scene. A *roll* involves a camera flipping an image of a person, object, or scene about, which is much more disorienting than the other kinds of shots. A *truck* (left or right) involves the horizontal movement of the camera and its support in front of a given scene; a *dolly-in* or *dolly-out* involves the actual movement of the camera and its support either toward or away from a scene; and an *arc* is a movement, semicircular in nature, of a camera and its support around a given scene.

❚ Figure 5.6
Orson Welles, frame from
Citizen Kane, 1941. This is
an example of deep focus
in which the details at the
end of the table are as
clear as the ones at the
front of the table. Note,
also, how the ice sculp-
tures frame the image and
almost seem to be mem-
bers of the party.

Each of these shots creates a different effect. For example, the pan is a kind of inspection of a terrain, the tilt is more focused and direct, and the roll disorients and surprises the viewer.

Deep and Shallow Focus

Deep focus refers to a large depth of field, in which objects close to the camera, as well as those a considerable distance from it, are in clear focus. This clarity imparts a very strong sense of realism to a scene. Orson Welles used deep focus to stunning effect in his masterpiece *Citizen Kane* (Figure 5.6). *Shallow focus*, which involves having only a small part of an image in focus, directs the attention of the viewer to something in particular, by having it in focus and everything else out of focus.

The Jump Cut

With the *jump cut,* the editor slices out the middle or some part of a sequence and cuts or "jumps" from one section of it to another. This process helps shape the rhythm of the scene and speed it up. We learn the convention of the jump cut from comic books. The artists cannot provide all the interven-

■ **FIGURE 5.7**
Detail from Gilbert Shelton's *The Fabulous Furry Freak Brothers*, "Getting Out the Vote." Filmmakers have learned a great deal about varying their shots from studying frames in comic strips.

ing shots, so they jump from one scene to another and allow us to fill in the gaps in our own imaginations via the process of psychological closure (Figure 5.7).

POSTMODERNISM'S IMPACT ON FILM

Postmodernism is difficult to define but is related to such trends and ideas as the blending of different styles and genres (often seen in buildings) and the depreciation of narratives (reflected in the mass media and in some philosophical thought). Thus, postmodern films tend to lack an easy-to-follow linear narrative structure. It's best to think of these films in terms of montage—the juxtaposing of images and fragments of narratives to generate responses from viewers without much regard for sequence and plot line, as we traditionally recognize them.

According to Jack Solomon, *Koyaanisqatsi*, a 1983 film by Godfrey Reggio, is a classic example of postmodernism. As Solomon writes in *The Signs of Our Times: The Secret Meanings of Everyday Life* (1990:213):

It has no characters, no dialogue, no words, no subtitles, no narrative, nor anything recognizable as a plot. Without commentary or overview, the cameras simply juxtapose such violently contrasting images from the natural and the industrialized worlds as Indian hieroglyphics, a slow-motion rocket launch, time-lapse photography of cloud patterns, scenic aerial views of the American Southwest, atomic blasts, shots of the litter-filled streets of New York, endless replays of the demolition of a decaying housing complex, scenes from Las Vegas . . .

The film also features a minimalist score by avant-garde composer Philip Glass that, as Solomon puts it, "pulses in rhythmic correlation with the imagery."

After eighty-seven minutes of "sensory assault," the film concludes by flashing some definitions of the term *koyaanisqatsi* on the screen. As Solomon recounts (1990:214), *koyaanisqatsi* is a Hopi term that means "1. crazy life, 2. life in turmoil, 3. life out of balance, 4. life disintegrating, 5. a state of life that calls for another way of living." The film uses a variety of images to generate this feeling in viewers and offers a filmic mosaic of the world suggesting that it is in turmoil and that life is chaotic. We can wonder whether *Koyaanisqatsi* is a mirror reflecting a society in a state of disintegration or is a kind of lamp projecting this view of the world, a view held by its maker but not necessarily an accurate portrayal of contemporary society.

In any case, *Koyaanisqatsi* and a number of films such as *Blue Velvet, Blade Runner, Crimes and Misdemeanors,* and *sex, lies and videotape* are generally held to be postmodern in nature. That is, they are thought—or so postmodernist theorists argue—to reflect the postmodern, nonlinear, image-crazy world in which we live.

THE POWER OF THE FILM IMAGE

When we see a film in a theater, we find ourselves "captives" (in a sense) in a large room with others, where we sit in darkness watching huge images on a gigantic screen. The very scale of these images itself has an impact; that is why you get a much different feeling when you see a film in a theater than you do when you see that same film in your home. And the quality of the audio system in the theater is also much better, which intensifies the experience.

But there is something about movies, wherever we see them, that also strikes responsive chords in us. It is the fact that we generally are watching stories featuring human beings, with whom we can empathize and to whom we often have (and often unconsciously) a sensual or erotic response. As Martin Esslin suggests in *The Age of Television* (1982:30):

■ FIGURE 5.8

Aristotle said that comedy is based on making men ridiculous. Could he have been thinking of Woody Allen's outfit in his film *Sleeper* (1973)?

> Drama is basically erotic. Actors give the spectators who watch them a great deal of pleasure simply by being interesting, memorable, or beautiful specimens of humanity. Quite apart from their artistic or intellectual accomplishments, actors are people who exhibit their physical presence to the public. . . . In a sense all actors are exhibitionists: they enjoy being seen, being found appealing and worth looking at. Conversely audiences of dramas are also, in a certain sense, voyeurs.

The power of this generally submerged and subliminal erotic relationship we have with actors and actresses is such that it is easy to identify with them and to internalize their values and beliefs. In some films, or at least in some scenes in films, a comic response rather than an erotic one is generated. This is the case in *Sleeper,* in which we find Woody Allen in an absurd costume (Figure 5.8).

There is an element of what is called *scopophilia* (loving by looking) at play here, which helps explain why facial expressions play so important a role in drama. We are all fascinated by others and want to know as much as we can about them, their personalities, their hidden selves. Thus, we scrutinize their facial expressions (and take note of everything else, I might add) as a means of getting to know characters. In discussing television, Esslin writes (1982: 29), "The ability of TV to transmit personality is, undoubtedly, the secret of its immense power. For human beings are insatiable in their interest about other human beings." The same could be said about films.

It may also be that the sense of isolation and separation many people feel in modern societies exacerbates their hunger for relationships (even if only mass-mediated pseudorelationships) and makes movies and television dramas much more important aspects of their lives than they might otherwise be. Social scientists use the term "para-social relationships" for the feeling many people have that they really know actors and actresses.

THE NATURE OF DRAMA

Films generally tell stories; that is, they are narratives in which we find characters pursuing their own interests, often in conflict with one another. Thus, the element of action is added to that of personality (and, often, demonstrates personality), enabling us to make a "willing suspension of disbelief" and enter into the drama, forgetting that we are spectators watching actors and actresses pretending to be certain characters doing various things. In dramas, there usually is a conflict (or many conflicts) between characters (who may be heroes and heroines and villains and villainesses) and a satisfactory resolution to the conflict.

The pacing of many films, the rapidity of the action sequences, and the nature of the dangers presented to the heroes and heroines excite us. Such excitement is inherent in films such as *Raiders of the Lost Ark* and others in that genre, in which one action scene leads to another one in rapid succession (Figure 5.9). These are very similar in structure to commercials full of quick cuts. The very rapidity of the cutting generates a sense of excitement.

In many respects, film and television dramas are like dreams, in which all kinds of remarkable things occur (Figure 5.10). According to Freudian theory, our dreams occur in the form of discontinuous images that we "put together" when we recall them, via a process known as *secondary elaboration*.

A dream would be very much like a series of jump cuts or comic strip panels, for which our minds fill in the gaps. What makes dreams (and films) powerful is that they are full of symbols that speak to repressed or uncon-

Steven Spielberg, *Raiders of the Lost Ark,* 1981. This film featured an almost endless sequence of life-threatening situations that the hero, Indiana Jones (Harrison Ford), had to overcome.

Ingmar Bergman, *The Seventh Seal,* 1956. Bergman's use of symbolism and the striking photography give this film a dream-like quality and incredible dramatic power.

scious elements in our psyches and that evoke powerful responses. Generally, these symbols have a sexual content that is hidden or masked by the processes of displacement and condensation. If there are erotic aspects to watching films and television, as Esslin suggests, there are even more powerful sexual aspects to our dreams—the dramas that we create in our own minds as we sleep. In our dreams, we are not only the producers and directors but also the actors and actresses.

CONCLUSIONS

Film is a very powerful and complex medium. In recent years, with the development of semiotics (often in alliance with psychoanalytic theory and Marxist theory), we have become interested in how films generate meaning for people and have discovered that it is a very complicated process. We used to think that a given film had a given meaning and that it was the function of the film critic to point out that meaning. Now we know that everyone doesn't interpret a given film the same way. What we see and get out of a film is related to what we know and have experienced in life.

Thus, if a film is full of parodies of other directors' work and includes allusions to historical events and we don't recognize the parodies or the allusions, we will not get as much out of that film as will someone who does recognize them. That is why it is now fashionable to talk about audiences "reading" films and to suggest that audiences must play a significant role in making sense of a film. The film does not bear the entire burden; instead, it cooperates with us, so to speak.

This shows why an understanding of the principles of visual communication is so important. When we study a film (or that important genre of film or television we call the commercial), the more we know about lighting and camera angles and kinds of shots and color and symbolism, the better we will be able to understand how it works and, finally, what is good and bad about it.

Of course, when we go to the movies simply to enjoy ourselves, we just watch the film and hope to be entertained by it. But later on, if we discuss the film with friends or study it, we can employ the repertoire of visual communication concepts we have learned to make sense of the film and our responses to it. It is true, also, that the more we know of how film (or any form of visual communication for that matter) works, the more our appreciation of film is enhanced. So the more you know, the more you can appreciate forms of visual communication—or literature, music, and all other art forms.

APPLICATIONS

1. Make a list of the five best films you've seen in the last year or so, ranked from one to five. What are your criteria for evaluating a film—that is, what makes a film "good"? Do you think certain criteria should be generally accepted, or are such things essentially a matter of opinion and personal taste? Compare your list with those of your classmates to see whether there is any agreement on which were the best films.

2. If you think a film is wonderful and a friend thinks the film is terrible, what is the "truth" of the matter? Is one of you likely to be correct and the other likely to be incorrect, or can you both be correct? Why is taste an unreliable guide to aesthetic judgments?

3. Videotape a film and then play it without the sound for a while, so that you can concentrate on such matters as facial expressions, lighting, editing, and kinds of shots. Rewind it and play it with sound. Do you have a better understanding of how the film was made and how it achieves its effects?

4. What makes a film a "classic"? In what ways do "classic" films differ from ordinary films?

5. Can you think of ways in which films have been influenced by television's visual techniques? Be specific about the films and the techniques.

6. Suppose you were asked to teach a course on contemporary American culture (since the 1960s). Which films would you use to give your students an understanding of our culture in all its variety? Justify your choices.

TELEVISION:
The Ever-Changing Mosaic

Essentially, television is more like radio than it is different from it. As with radio, the concept of flow is all-important; the product of both media is continuous and continuing, with both the smaller unit of the show and the larger unit of the day's or evening's programming. Moreover, because of the relatively poor quality of the televised image (as compared with theatrical film), TV depends heavily on its audio component. The curved screen, the lack of definition and contrast, the difficulties of broadcast reception, all work to minimize the effectiveness of the TV image. Visually, the density of information is low, which is made up for in part by a relatively compressed density of programming and sequencing. The segue and lead-in of radio are also of prime significance in the grammar of television: dead space and dead time are to be avoided at all costs: the flow must continue.

– JAMES MONACO,
HOW TO READ A FILM

If you spend four hours a day watching television (approximately the national average), by the time you reach age sixty-five, you will have spent about nine years in front of the "boob tube." Was that the best expenditure you could have made of those nine years? In this chapter, we explore television's curious power and investigate the medium everyone "loves to hate."

THE TELEVISION IMAGE

Watching television is considerably different from watching film. The film image is like a discrete photograph, loaded with information and very high in resolution. When we watch a film, we see twenty-four of these frames per second, each of which appears very briefly and then is followed by another. Because of the lingering afterimage, we get the effect or, should we say, have the illusion of motion.

The television image is altogether different. It is best described as a mosaic, made up of a large quantity of dots that are constantly changing. As Marshall McLuhan put it in *Understanding Media: The Extensions of Man* (1965:313):

> With TV, the viewer is the screen. He is bombarded with light impulses that James Joyce called the "Charge of the Light Brigade" that imbues his "soulskin with sobconscious inklings." The TV image is visually low in data. The TV image is not a still shot. It is not photo in any sense, but a ceaselessly forming contour of things limned by the scanning finger. . . . The TV image offers some three million dots per second to the receiver. From these he accepts only a few dozen each instant, from which to make an image.

113

▌FIGURE 6.1
Photo of television image at 1/1000 second.

▌FIGURE 6.2
Photo of television image at 1/500 second.

McLuhan probably underestimated the number of dots we use to make images, but his point is correct: a television image is a constantly changing mosaic of dots, and viewers must make sense of them (Figures 6.1, 6.2, and 6.3). We can do so with great facility and ease, but the point is, we *must* do so.

It is this difference between the amount of data given by the television image and the screen image that led McLuhan to suggest that differences in media are more important than the differences in the programs or genres they carry. As he put it, "the medium is the message." McLuhan has a highly controversial theory that distinguishes between "hot" media and "cool" media. A *hot medium*, he tells us (1965:22), "is one that extends one single sense in 'high definition.' High definition is being well filled with data." When there is high definition, McLuhan adds, there is low participation. A *cool medium*, on the other hand, has low definition, offers relatively few data, and fosters high participation.

A list of hot and cool media, as McLuhan sees things, follows.

Hot	*Cool*
Film	Television
Radio	Telephone
Photograph	Cartoon
Printed word	Speech
Lecture	Seminar
Book	Dialogue

❚ **Figure 6.3**
Photo of television image at 1/125 second.

The television image, because it is so low in data relative to the film image, is cool and encourages (or should we say requires) participation and attention.

The very nature of the television image, then, has a significance and an impact on viewers. According to McLuhan, television is more involving than film, requires more effort from the viewer, and is used in different ways by viewers. However, studies reveal that people do not, in fact, always watch television with undiluted attention; the set is on in a lighted room, and people watching it often converse with one another, eat, read, and do all kinds of things. And viewers watch more than three and one-half hours of television per day in America. (The television set is on almost seven hours per day in a typical home.)

From McLuhan's perspective, this is important because he believed that the medium of television has altered our sense ratios, or patterns of perception, and that this development has had a profound impact on us (and people in other countries as well, because this alteration varies from culture to culture). As he wrote (1965:45):

> There is . . . no way of refusing to comply with the new sense ratios of the TV image. But the effect of the entry of the TV image will vary from culture to culture in accordance with the existing sense ratios in each culture. In audio-tactile Europe TV has intensified the visual sense, spurring them toward American styles of packaging and dressing. In America, the intensely visual culture, TV has opened the doors of audio-tactile perception to the non-visual world of spoken languages and food and the plastic arts.

McLuhan's theories were very controversial when he launched them in the early 1960s. Now they are not so frequently discussed; but they explain a good deal and, if taken with a grain of salt, help us understand why different media affect us the way they do.

THE TELEVISION SCREEN

Television Versus Movie Screens

When we go to the movies, we sit in a large room and watch huge images on a very big screen. Movie screens vary in shape—depending on how the films are shot—but they are all large, and some are even gigantic. The television screen, on the other hand, is relatively small. Many sets have a twelve-inch screen (measured diagonally), though the most common size screen is a good deal larger than that, ranging from nineteen to twenty-five inches. There are even larger screens, but they are much more expensive and not as widely used.

The small television screen means that images are relatively small, which is why many people argue that television is a close-up medium. As Martin Esslin writes in *The Age of Television* (1982:30,32):

> Television is the most voyeuristic of all communication media, not only because it provides more material in an unending stream of images and in the form most universally acceptable to the total population, but also because it is the most intimate of the dramatic media. In the theatre, the actors are relatively remote from the audience, and the dramatic occasion is public. In the cinema, also a public occasion gathering a large audience into a single room, the actors are nearer to the spectators than in the theatre, but in close-ups they are larger than life. Television is seen at close range and in a more private context. *The close-up of the television performer is on a scale that most nearly approximates direct human contact.* [My italics]

Thus, the close-up image on television, uniquely, gives us the illusion of being with others, which has profound psychological implications. It is television, more than any other medium, that can generate pseudocompanionship, an electronic intimacy that is illusory and unreal.

From this perspective, our sense of "knowing" characters on television and our erotic feelings about them should be much stronger than with characters from films, especially if we watch television programs that are serial in nature and expose us to these characters daily (or weekly) for extended periods of time.

■ FIGURE 6.4
This drawing shows the
A-B axis. It is a simplifica-
tion of the Johnnie Walker
advertisement shown in
Figure 2.13.

■ FIGURE 6.5
This drawing shows the
Z-axis. It is a simplification
of the Johnnie Walker
advertisement shown in
Figure 3.15.

The small screen also means that action on television takes place on the Z-axis, the axis that extends from the viewer through the television screen and that is perpendicular to it. On a huge film screen, action can move horizontally across the screen (on what is known as the *A-B axis*) and not lose impact. On the tiny television set, things are different. The only way to deal with large spaces is via the Z-axis, which means action generally moves toward and away from the viewer. The viewer is therefore more directly involved in action. Figures 6.4 and 6.5 show the difference between A-B axis action and Z-axis action.

It is possible to suggest, then, that the small size of the television screen involves viewers in two ways: via the close-up, which approximates human conversational distance, and via the Z-axis, which situates viewers so that action almost always takes place moving toward or away from them.

Watching a film on television is different, then, from watching the same film in a theater. The film does not focus as directly on the viewer and the Z-axis or rely so heavily on close-ups, so that the impact of the film, when it is seen on the television screen, is different from its impact when seen in a theater. The quality of the image is also different, and this has an effect on the film's impact. The film image, which is very powerful and full of information, is turned into a television image and thus diluted.

This does not mean we cannot get a good deal of pleasure from watching a film on television; the incredible development of the videocassette rental industry for films shows that people like to watch films on their home systems. But they are not having the same experience as seeing the film in a theater, with a large screen and a powerful stereophonic audio system. (The amount of money people save on tickets and baby-sitters by renting video-cassettes likely is of primary importance; convenience may also be a factor.)

Talking Heads

There is an element of conventional wisdom in the television industry about avoiding programs with "talking heads." If all one has is a program with no variety of camera shots and the talk from these talking heads is dull and uninteresting, the program will, indeed, be dull.

But it isn't as simple as that. Many programs that involve, for the most part, talking heads are extremely interesting and diverting. On the Public Broadcasting System, for example, two of the most popular programs for many years have been "Washington Week in Review" and "Wall Street Week." In the first program, several reporters sit around a table and talk about politics, and in the second, financial advisors talk about money. There is not much in the way of action; but because the topics of these two programs—politics and money—are of great interest to many people, there doesn't have to be any action. In fact, any action would be counter-productive.

In the summer of 1987, the Iran-Contra hearings took place before joint House and Senate committees; and millions of people watched, transfixed, as a collection of incredible characters came before the cameras to tell fantastic stories about their actions and activities. These recalled the McCarthy hearings of the 1950s and the Watergate hearings of the 1970s—other occasions when millions were enthralled by "talking heads."

During the Iran-Contra hearings, witnesses contradicted one another and revealed amazing things about what was going on in the White House and how U.S. foreign policy was being conducted. The hearings "created" a new American hero (at least for some people), Oliver North, whose hairstyle was promptly imitated by large numbers of young men and whose appearance also seems to have had, at least in the short run, benefits for the Contras and military recruiting.

In these hearings (and in all talking heads programs), the camera played an important role and was very active—scanning the committee, zooming in on witnesses who were testifying, showing important evidence that had been enlarged and posted on the walls of the committee hearing room. An active camera can generate energy and force viewers to think in certain ways (thus, the zoom-in suggests that we pay attention because something important is going on). The camera work can add an element of drama to a given program.

If one of the functions of television is to bring personalities to viewers, there's nothing in the talking head format that prevents this from being done. In the final analysis, it is the quality of the people who are talking and what they have to say that is crucial. And a great number of formats on television employ little more than talking heads: game shows, talk shows, interviews, and political speeches.

TELEVISION GENRES

Three television genres are particularly interesting in terms of visual communication: the commercial, the news program, and music videos. The commercial is also important because it is the cash cow that finances television. In fact, some media critics have suggested that television programming exists mainly to furnish an audience for the commercials, the most important genre carried by the medium.

We must make a distinction between a medium, such as television, and its program genres: commercials, news shows, sports programs, science fiction programs, talk shows, soap operas, situation comedies, crime shows, and so on. Many critics pay little attention to the impact of a medium on a genre, which means they neglect a matter of considerable importance. It is as much an oversimplification to argue that "the program is the message" as it is to argue that "the medium is the message." We must always keep in mind the conventions of genres when we talk about television shows.

The Commercial

In 1997, advertisers spent around $180 billion on all media and approximately $30 billion on television. That translates into an enormous number of commercials. As a result of the high cost of airtime, commercials are getting shorter and shorter, which means they must compress their messages into thirty or even fifteen seconds. This compression obviously has an impact on the visual aspects of the commercial.

One thing that the commercial did was to get rid of (in most cases) the establishing shot—the long shot that gives viewers a sense of context. Films traditionally used establishing shots regularly. We would see an extreme long shot of a building; then the camera would pan along the street to the building, up the building to a window, and into the window where the action would begin. The commercial plunges viewers right into the middle of the action and gets them involved immediately. Films have now adopted this convention and, like commercials, now frequently "start in the middle."

Many commercials can be described as microdramas, in which a traditional plot is compressed to thirty seconds. In these microdramas, the product is a miraculous agent that resolves problems and allows the characters to, we surmise, live happily ever after (Figure 6.6).

To sell as quickly and convincingly as possible, actors and actresses in commercials use a great deal of facial expression and body language. If you turn off the sound and simply watch commercials, you can see that many of the characters really exaggerate their facial expressions and body language. The exaggeration counters the brevity of their performances and the disbelief that viewers bring to commercials. The performers also use their voices, all kinds of props, their sexuality, humor, and anything else they can to convince viewers to buy a given product or service.

Analyzing the Commercial

Television exists, it has been suggested, to provide audiences for companies selling goods and services. Thus, the commercial is television's most important genre—and, in certain respects, its most interesting. Commercials cost an enormous amount of money to produce and to air. The people who make commercials are some of the best and most creative individuals in the advertising and film and video world. We can learn a great deal, then, from studying these minidramas to see how they obtain their effects. What follows is a list of some of the more important topics to consider in analyzing commercials. Consider the storyboard in Figure 6.7, as well as the one in Figure 6.6, while you read this list.

NARRATIVE STRUCTURE. What happens in the commercial? What is its plot—if a plot exists? What techniques are used to captivate viewers? Are there flashbacks or flash-forwards? Is there a narrator? Is there action? Is there conflict?

CHARACTERS. Who are the characters in the commercial? What are their characteristics? What relationships seem to exist among them? Are they appealing? Are they funny? Are there hunks and glamor girls? If so, what function do they have? How are we supposed to relate to these characters? What about their faces (and use of facial expression), the style and color of their hair, the shape of their bodies, their age, the clothes they wear, and the possessions they have? What kind of voices do they have? How might they help sell the product or service being advertised?

DIALOGUE. What kind of language is used? What techniques of persuasion are used to sell viewers: humor, scare tactics and the generation of anxiety, sexuality and "seductiveness," appeals to authority or to vanity, pleading, and so on?

▌ Figure 6.7
Storyboard for "1984" microdrama commercial by Chiat/Day Advertising, Los Angeles.

SETTING. Where does the action take place? When does it take place? What significance does the setting have? Are there any props of importance—furniture, paintings, machines, gadgets, cars, and so on?

VISUALS. What kinds of shots are found in the commercial? Is there a variety of shots: close-ups, extreme close-ups, long shots, and so on? What shot angles are used, and what effect do they have?

What about the editing? How is the commercial cut? Is there hardly any cutting at all, or is there a great deal of quick cutting? If there is quick cutting, what impact does it have? Are such things as dissolves, distortion, compression, or fade-outs used? What impact do these phenomena have?

Also, how is color used? What colors are found in the commercial, and what role do these colors play? What kinds of effects are generated by the colors? How is the color related to the lighting?

VIEWERS' STORE OF KNOWLEDGE. What generally held beliefs, attitudes, values, ideas, myths, heroic archetypes, and so on are reflected in the commercial?

CHECKLIST FOR ANALYZING TELEVISION COMMERCIALS

The following checklist focuses on the most important elements to keep in mind when viewing and analyzing television commercials.

The Narrative Structure

1. What happens in the commercial? What is the narrative line?
2. What dramatic techniques are used in the commercial? Is there humor? Surrealism?
3. Is there a narrator? If so, what is the narrator's function?
4. Is there action? What is the significance of the action?
5. Is there conflict? If so, what kind? And how is it resolved?

The Characters

6. Who are the characters? What roles do they play?
7. What do the characters in the commercial look like? Consider their facial features, their hair color and style, their bodies, their use of body language, the clothes they wear, and so on.
8. What relationship seems to exist among the characters?
9. What are the demographics of the characters in terms of age, sex, race, ethnicity, educational level, occupation, and so on?
10. What are the voices of the characters like? Do they have accents?
11. How do the attributes of the characters in the narrative help sell the product?

The Dialogue

12. What kind of language is used?
13. Does the commercial use rhetorical devices such as metaphors, associations, or alliteration? What about exaggeration, comparison and contrast, jingles, or humor?

The Setting

14. Where does the action of the commercial take place?
15. What significance does the setting have? How is the setting used to give viewers certain impressions?
16. Are any props of importance used?

The Visual Images and Sound

17. What kinds of shots are used? How many different scenes are there in the commercial?
18. How is the commercial edited? Are there numerous quick cuts? Lingering dissolves? Zooms? How are close-ups used?
19. How is color used?
20. How is lighting used?
21. Are there any intertextual elements in the commercial, such as reference to well-known films, works of literature, and the like?
22. How is sound used? Is there music? If so, what kind, and what effect might it have?

The Viewers

23. How does the commercial use information viewers already have to sell them on the product or service being advertised?
24. How does the commercial relate to popularly held beliefs, myths, ideas, attitudes, values, and archetypes?

The Product

25. What function does the product have? How do people use it?
26. What does the product and the commercial tell us about social and political considerations? For example, does it reflect problems such as alienation, anxiety, generational conflict, stereotyped thinking, or boredom?

Because commercials are so compressed, they are forced to draw on and use information and ideas their viewers already have in their heads. The primary function of the commercial is to generate a response, to create "desire," not to convey information. Commercials make use of the stock of information we all have picked up, often through our experiences and the mass media, for their own purposes.

It is useful to think of commercials as "sign systems" and to consider every aspect of a commercial as a sign to be interpreted. Thus, all of the topics discussed in this book can be used to interpret and understand the fascinating (and often irritating) art form we know as the commercial.

Television News

News programs (as well as documentaries and certain videos) are at the opposite end of the "disbelief spectrum." Numerous surveys indicate, for example, that large numbers of Americans get most of their news from television news programs and think that the news shows are more believable than stories in newspapers. We know, however, that while the camera doesn't lie, the person who controls the camera can "lie" or, at least, determine what is presented to the viewing public.

In a famous study of a 1950s parade in Chicago for General Douglas MacArthur after he had been fired by President Truman, Kurt and Gladys Engel Lang showed that what was presented on television news programs was quite different from what really went on. The actual parade was a rather dull affair, and not too many people were there; but, by using only certain shots, the television news directors led viewers to believe that it was an exciting event with mobs of people. As we noted in the discussion of photography, cameras don't lie, but liars use cameras.

News programs are also interesting for those interested in visual communications because they use a large number of graphics, captions, and similar devices. Television news is visual and aural; but there is still a need for the written word and for various kinds of signs, charts, and graphs, because they can show relationships very well and compress a great deal of complex information into a relatively simple visual display.

The news program (at least the national news) is generally a very sober affair that strives for realism. But events on television news programs often are dramatized so that they entertain as well. In other words, the producer of a news program can make the news "exciting" by injecting dramatic elements into stories—who is winning or losing, who is lying or telling the truth, or what important consequences will stem from a given event. Visually, national newscasts all have a similar look: we see the anchor or anchors sitting at a desk with screens in the background. The anchor narrates the news, and the program switches back and forth between the anchor and the field reporters, who are usually shown on screen, interviewing important figures or showing some scene of consequence.

Because television is a visual medium, many critics have suggested that television news focuses on stories that have a visual dimension to them and neglect many important stories that don't. Whatever the case, the typical national newscast runs for thirty minutes (with six or more minutes taken up with commercials), and it cannot go into great depth for any story, which is why some media analysts have suggested that television news is essentially a headline service. Viewers interested in details, background, and analysis must go to a print medium, such as a newspaper or magazine (or to a program like "The News Hour with Jim Lehrer" on public television).

Televised Hearings

Televised hearings, court proceedings (such as the O. J. Simpson trial), and similar events represent one of the more important new genres in television. These hearings have often played an important role in our political order, affecting the careers of important politicians and, at times, even presidents.

Televised hearings generally attempt to avoid manipulating images with camera work, lighting, and so on, but sometimes, by chance, the camera placement has significant effects. In *Picture Perfect: The Art and Artifice of Public Image-Making,* Kiku Adatto recounts a story in which the filmmaker Steven Spielberg was visiting Washington during the Iran-Contra hearings. Adatto writes (1993:13):

> As he watched the hearings with some Democratic congressmen, he offered them a lesson in camera angles. "Watch this," Spielberg said, as he turned down the sound and directed the congressmen's attention to [Colonel Oliver] North's image on the screen. "The camera on North is shooting up, from about four inches below his eyes. This is the way they shot Gary Cooper in the western, *High Noon,* to make him look like a hero." When the camera panned to the committee members questioning North, Spielberg pointed out, the lighting was dim. Seen at a distance, they looked sinister. Spielberg told the assembled Democrats: "It doesn't matter what Oliver North says. He has already won the battle because he looks like a hero and everyone else looks like a villain."

We can see, then, that matters which might seem to be trivial, such as camera angles and lighting, play an important role in hearings and similar media events, because images often convey messages to viewers that are more significant than what is being said by the person being videotaped.

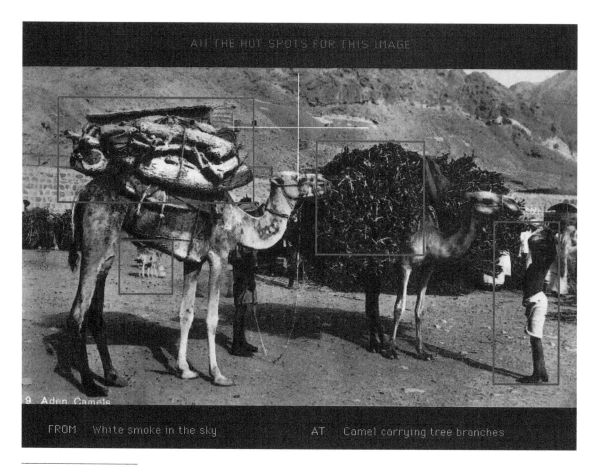

▊ **FIGURE 6.8**
This image comes from *Slippery Traces* by video artist George Legrady.

▊ **FIGURE 6.9**
Lynn Hershman, still from "Eyewitness," 1984. This image has surrealistic elements in its use of various pairs of eyes.

Music Videos

This genre is particularly interesting for students of visual communication because we find that MTV has a particular look to it. The music videos broadcast on television are, in fact, commercials for the recordings produced by various musical groups. Depending on the available money and the artistic inclinations of the producer, the videos generally either show the band making the song or turn the song into some kind of a dramatic piece.

What is interesting about music videos is that so many of them have surrealistic qualities. *Surrealism* is a visual style that is dreamlike and nonlinear (full of flash-forwards and flashbacks), makes use of fantastic images and distorted perspectives, and is full of special effects (Figures 6.8, 6.9, and 6.10). The term *surrealism* comes from painting and describes the work of a group of highly experimental artists such as Joan Miró, Salvador Dalí, André Breton, and René Magritte, who worked in the 1920s (and later) and who wanted to represent the unconscious mind with their paintings.

We find surrealistic elements in many music videos—a surprising combination of avant-garde visual aesthetics and rather ordinary, formulaic musical aesthetics. One of the problems with music television is that after watching it for an hour or so, it tends to blur in your mind. There's been so much visual excitement that you suffer from a bad case of "information overload."

These music videos, one might argue, take the experimentalism and vitality found in the commercial and push these phenomena to their furthest limits. They have, in turn, greatly influenced the look of regular commercials and also have impacted the psyches of the teenagers (and others) who watch them.

In her essay "The Look of the Sound," Pat Aufderheide describes how these videos relate to young people in America (1987:118):

> With nary a reference to cash or commodities, music videos cross the consumer's gaze as a series of mood states. They trigger moods such as nostalgia, regret, anxiety, confusion, dread, envy, admiration, pity, titillation—attitudes at one remove from primal expressions such as passion, ecstasy, and rage. The moods often express a lack, an incompletion, an instability, a searching for location. In music videos, those feelings are carried on flights of whimsy, extended journeys into the arbitrary.

These music videos, Aufderheide argues, reflect a basic tension found in American youth culture—a sense of instability and incompleteness. These feelings push young people into a quest to "buy and belong" that forces them to "become a piece of the action in a continuous performance." Is it healthy, one might ask, to have young people, who are searching for stable identities, spend so much time watching a genre that is full of discontinuities and

∎ FIGURE 6.10
Lynn Hershman, still from
"Birdie," 1987. This surrealistic image was created
using a Proteus computer.

∎ FIGURE 6.10
Lynn Hershman, still from "Birdie," 1987. This surrealistic image was created using a Proteus computer.

random chaos, as well as images that, all too often, are sexist, sadistic, and excessively violent?

One of the more interesting aspects of music videos is that their visual elements are used to enhance the music, rather than the music being used to enhance the visual images—the opposite of what is found in films and television. The music is what is basic. These videos create narratives (stories) that often use innovative choreography, costuming, animation, and avant-garde editing techniques (quick cuts, unusual montages, hand-held cameras, dramatic colors and lighting, and so on). In short, music videos represent an exciting, distinctive genre that dramatizes music, often in visually interesting and arresting ways.

VIDEO ARTISTS

It is hard, at times, to know where to draw the line between what we call commercial television and video art. The video artists, like all artists, have their private visions and use video to make personal statements, to create videos that they think are beautiful and thought-provoking. Unlike commercial television, these videos are not meant to please the general public, though videos sometimes are shown on television stations (generally public television). They are often highly imaginative, can be experimental in form (in the way they manipulate images, color, music, and narrative structure), and frequently have sociological and ideological dimensions to them.

Ironically, music television and other television borrows from these video artists—in the same way that the surrealists influenced other artists and impacted other media. The moral is that art styles and movements have an impact and influence that is quite widespread.

ZAPPING OR CHANNEL SURFING

The final irony, relative to the television image, stems from the development of the remote-control channel switcher. Increasingly large numbers of people use these channel switchers for "zapping" or channel surfing, a process by which they jump, back and forth, from channel to channel. Estimates suggest that about a third of television watchers zap regularly and that more than 50 percent of teenagers do so.

What this means is that people are watching not so much television programs as television itself. (This is a big problem for advertising agencies, which are selling audiences to advertisers. If people flip at the first sign of a commercial, or even before that, the whole television advertising industry is in trouble.) Not only is the television screen a mosaic, but people are also turning television itself into a kind of mosaic and simultaneously watching (to the extent that the term *watching* applies) a dozen or more programs at the same time.

This reduces television to its elemental form—visual images—and people who zap essentially turn television into a set of visual images (and auditory stimuli) at the expense of program form and continuity. We have a micro-mosaic reaching its audience in the form of what we might call macromosaic, a huge surrealistic collection of bits and pieces of many different programs and stories that become a person's television program. People who zap make their own television programs out of the programming available at a given time—an electronic montage. Thanks to the remote-control device, we can all become video artists.

CONCLUSIONS

Television is the medium everyone loves to hate. It has been described as a "vast wasteland" and is the object of endless condemnation by elitists, many of whom take pride in never watching it. It is also the object of countless studies by psychologists, sociologists, and other social scientists, who investigate its effect on everything from our family lives to our sex lives to our political behavior.

One of the most important shortcomings of many studies of television is that they pay no attention to the visual and aesthetic aspects of the medium.

The basic model for most studies comes from social psychology and is concerned with the impact of television on attitudes, beliefs, and values—which can then be used to predict everything from consumer behavior to voting behavior. This model, which neglects the power of images, sound, and other aesthetic factors (such as the kinds of shots used, the cutting, and so on), is simplistic and not adequate to deal with television in all of its complexity.

Fortunately, this emphasis is changing; and as interest in visual communication progresses, we can hope that new and better ways of studying television will emerge.

APPLICATIONS

1. Watch commercials without the sound so that you can pay attention to their technical aspects. What do you find of interest?

2. Assume you have been asked to create a commercial for some product. Create a storyboard for the projected commercial (with six or eight frames), and be prepared to explain to a potential client why you did what you did. How will your commercial help sell the product?

3. Create a new television genre by mixing various television genres, and write a one-paragraph description of the show, for newspapers, that would summarize the show for potential viewers. You can use up to three genres. In what way is your new genre distinctive and unique? Why would audiences like it?

4. Tape three network news programs and compare them in terms of the order of topics, the topics covered, and related concerns. Are there important similarities? If so, why? Are there important differences? If so, how do you explain this? (You can do the same for local news programs also. See if you can figure out how the show with the highest ratings differs from its competitors.)

5. Make a list of the topics covered in a network news program, and compare it with the first page of *The New York Times*. What do you find? Is television news just a "headline" service? What does that mean?

6. Using everything you've learned about visual communication, analyze a music video that you find interesting. Consider such matters as the images, the cutting, the lighting, the use of color, the way performers are shot, the way women are shown (and their roles), the way men are shown (and their roles), the lyrics, and anything else that you think is of interest. What factors contribute to the video's appeal? And why have music videos been so successful overall?

7

COMICS, CARTOONS, AND ANIMATION:
The Development of an Art Form

Comics have evolved from lowly "kid's stuff" appearing in newspapers into graphic novels and animated films of considerable power and brilliance. They are also valuable repositories of our social and cultural beliefs and practices.

THE COMIC STRIP

Comic strips have been prominent features of American newspapers since the early 1900s, and some media scholars have suggested that, in many respects, the comic strip is an American idiom. Describing the comic strip as an American medium would be more proper. Over the years, a huge number of comic strips have been created, many of which are now seen as "classics" and are being reprinted in large art books.

We now recognize that the comic strip has an aesthetic quality of its own and that the strips are important repositories of our values and beliefs. For this reason, historians and sociologists have made increasing use of the comics as a kind of documentary record of American culture—especially in the early part of the twentieth century. Many comic strips lasted fifty or sixty years; in some cases, a strip has been kept going after the original artist died by bringing in a different artist. This is the case with *Blondie*, which started in 1930 and still is being published.

Normal dialogue appears in balloons with an unbroken outline, with the tail pointing to the speaker. A perforated line indicates whispering. If the words are written in very small letters within a big balloon, it means the speaker is astonished or ashamed. A cry has a spiky outline, and the famous "telephone voice" has a zig-zag shape, with a zig-zag arrow disappearing into the telephone. Balloons indicating cold or conceited voices have little icicles sprouting from their undersides. Thought balloons are connected with the thinker by a series of little circles which look like bubbles, and if a speech balloon has a little arrow pointing outside the picture, the speaker is "off."

–RHEINHOLD REITBERGER AND WOLFGANG FUCHS, COMICS: ANATOMY OF A MASS MEDIUM

Reading the Comics

A *comic strip* can be defined as a form of pictorial art that has the following attributes:

1. Continuing characters
2. Frames that show the action
3. Dialogue in balloons (generally speaking)

Although we call them "comics" or "the funnies," there are many comic strips that are serious—so the term really is misleading. (The French use the term "designed bands," which implies that not all comics are humorous.) In fact, many of our greatest comic strips—*Dick Tracy, Little Orphan Annie, Buck Rogers, Tarzan*—are not humorous.

We can make a distinction between comics and cartoons: cartoons do not have continuing characters or dialogue shown in balloons. And some cartoons—political ones—are not always funny or meant to make people laugh, though many are humorous as well as critical.

There are, it turns out, a number of conventions we have to learn if we are to read the comics correctly. Let's look at them.

1. *The way characters are drawn.* In some comics, the style is realistic. But in others, it is highly stylized and meant to be funny; these characters have big noses, big ears, silly looks on their faces, and so on. The way the characters are drawn is a clue as to how to classify the strip—as funny or as serious.
2. *Facial expression.* Being a visual art, comics make considerable use of facial expression to show the feelings or emotional states of the various characters. Exaggerated facial expression is one way comic strip artists can inject humor into their strips.
3. *The role of balloons.* Comic strip artists use various methods to let us know how to respond to the dialogue of the characters. Sometimes, the words are shown in heavy print or in some other typeface. We often find exclamation marks used. There is another convention that is important here: thoughts are shown in scalloped balloons, and so comic strip artists can show what people are saying and thinking by using different kinds of balloons. Sound effects are often shown in zig-zagged balloons, which gives the artists one more way of generating effects.
4. *Movement lines.* Artists show movement and speed by using lines that indicate movement, and sometimes puffs of smoke to show how fast someone or something is moving.

5. *Panels at the bottom or top of the frame.* These panels are used to maintain continuity and to tell readers what to expect or what is going on at a given moment.
6. *The setting.* A given setting provides readers with a sense of what is going on and how seriously to take things.
7. *The action.* Each frame in a comic strip is the equivalent of a frame in a film, except that dialogue is shown in the comic strip, thoughts are revealed, and narration is provided through the printed word. The comic strip provides points of action that readers must fill in or complete in their own minds—quite similar to the "jump cut" of film.

Comic strips are often collaborations between writers and artists, though the old humorous comic strips generally were drawn and written by the same person. The artists who draw these strips use a variety of shots and shot angles in telling their stories. The artists must be mindful of the strip or the page (in the case of comic books) and make certain that they maintain visual interest by varying the kinds of shots and shot angles. (In this respect, the storyboards used in planning television commercials are very much like comic books: the storyboards show six or eight basic shots and indicate the dialogue that goes with each shot.)

As we grow up and become accustomed to reading the comics, we learn the various conventions connected with this medium. As with film, you have to learn how to "read" comics to be able to understand them fully.

Reading the comics, then, is not as simple as we might think. In addition to the various conventions we have to master, we must keep in mind that there is a complicated interplay between the visual elements of the comic strip and the linguistic ones. As Roger Sabin points out in *Adult Comics: An Introduction* (1993:9):

> A strip does not "happen" in the words, or the pictures, but somewhere in-between, in what is sometimes known as "the marriage of text and image." The strips may just be a mix of words and pictures, but the permutations of the two are almost endless—limited only by the imaginations of the creators. In short, strips have their own aesthetic: they are a language with their own grammar, syntax and punctuation. They are not some hybrid form halfway between "literature" and "art" (whatever those words might mean), but a medium in their own right.

Sabin's point is important, because many critics see the comics as, by definition, childish subliterature. That is, because we start reading comics when we are young children, many critics assume that comics must be childish. These critics are unaware that the comics are a distinctive medium and that

the mixture of images and words found in the comics has enormous resonance and power. Comics are a wonderful medium for telling stories—and
for teaching—and, in fact, the two often go together.

The Power of the Comic Strip

Why is this simple medium so powerful? For one thing, we spend many
years with comic strips and their characters. *Peanuts,* for example, started in
1950, and so many people have been following that strip for close to fifty
years. The more we follow the strip, the more significance various events that
happen in it have for us, because these events relate to the characters and
their personalities, and we have been observing both for long periods of time.
The comic strip is an iterative (repetitive) medium or "art form," as some put
it. Thus, the more we follow it, the more it means to us, until finally, as in
the case of *Peanuts,* its characters merge into our folklore and, in a curious
way, into our lives.

So the comic strip (or certain ones, at least) involves us for long periods
of time, even though we may read a given episode in a matter of seconds. In
addition, the comic strip has the power to create fantastic and fascinating
personalities, with whom we become "involved." In certain humorous ones,
we find personalities who spend decades "locked" in comedic combat with
one another—Beetle Bailey and Sarge in *Beetle Bailey,* Krazy Kat and Offissa
Pupp in *Krazy Kat,* and the Spook and the Jailors in *The Wizard of Id,* to
name just a few.

The great characters in comic strips develop their personalities over many
years, and we develop attachments to these characters and expectations
about them. Think of *Doonesbury* and its remarkable cast of characters,
who, year after year, keep appearing and reappearing in various guises and
situations.

The remarkable capacity of the comic strip to generate memorable characters is another reason comics are so powerful. We continually search for
personalities with whom we can identify (and to whom we can relate, even
if only through a medium). Thus, the comic strip, which can generate personalities who have extraordinarily long lives (as fictional characters go), has
much more impact on people than we might imagine.

In addition, the art style of some cartoons is extremely expressive and
often quite individualistic. (A French scholar, Robert Benayoun, even wrote
a book, *Black and White in the Comics,* which deals with the visual attributes
of the comic strip.) The use of grotesques (visually and psychologically) gives
the comic strip a unique power. The *grotesque* is an art style that uses exaggerated and often distorted physical characteristics to make a point. The

The Fabulous Furry Freak Brothers © Rip Off Press, Inc.

physical ugliness of grotesques is often allied, especially in the work of *Dick Tracy* creator Chester Gould, with their moral ugliness and criminality. Indeed, Gould created a veritable bestiary of criminal characters, such as Flat Top and the Mole, with whom he peopled his strip (Figure 7.1).

Psychologically, comics are filled with grotesques in the sense that we find numerous monomaniacs, obsessives, and single-minded types—who live only to scrounge their next meal, to escape from prison, to harass some character, or whatever. Most of these grotesques are found in strips where their obsessive quality becomes amusing and makes possible humor based on frustrating them. In some cases, we have momentary monomania—as in *Peanuts,* where Lucy congenitally fails to catch fly balls or snatches the football away just before Charlie Brown can kick it.

▌ **FIGURE 7.1**

(a) Chester Gould, *Dick Tracy.* This was one of the classic American strips, which featured a variety of grotesque-looking criminals. *(b)* The frames from Gilbert Shelton's *Tricky Prickears* parody *Dick Tracy.*

THE CARTOON

A *cartoon* is usually confined to one frame and does not have continuous characters, though it may use certain types over and over again (or, in the case of political cartoons, which are often not meant to be funny, certain political figures). The cartoon uses not balloons but captions underneath the frame to make its point. There are two types of cartoons: humorous cartoons (Figure 7.2), which often satirize conventions in a given society as well as certain character types, and political cartoons (Figures 7.3 and 7.4), which make a point about some political situation and which may or may not be funny.

The cartoon often relies heavily on information known to readers and thus functions by striking a responsive chord—by making us see something we didn't see before or recognize the cupidity and stupidity of humans and their institutions. Sometimes they can be used to provide valuable information in an amusing and nonthreatening manner (Figure 7.5). Cartoonists also may develop a recognizable "line" or style and a stance or point of view.

Many of the common techniques of humor are available to the cartoonist—who can set characters up and manipulate them for comic effect. Cartoonists use techniques such as revelation of ignorance, mistakes, exaggeration, co-incidence, satire, parody, and reversals. Therefore, although the elements of the cartoon are rather simple, the possibilities for expression are almost limitless.

L. C. Gregg in the Atlanta *Constitution*.

FOR PRESIDENT!

█ **FIGURE 7.3**
Philipon, "The Pears," *Le Charivari*, January 17, 1831. The artist used the image of a pear, playing on his face and physique to caricature France's King Louis-Philippe. Censors of the king eventually forbade artists to draw any pearlike figures.

Visual Humor in Cartoons

A number of important techniques of visual humor can be used in cartoons.

EXAGGERATION. Here the artist makes funny drawings in which feet are very big, noses are elongated, bodies are very large (relative to the size of heads or simply in general), ears stick out, and so on. Exaggeration is a standard

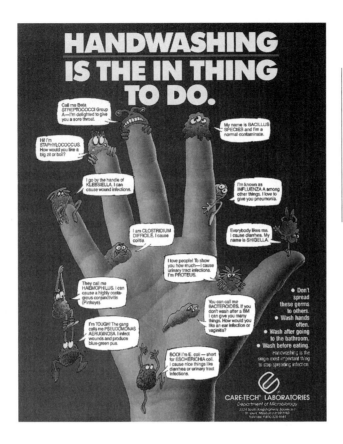

technique used by humorists; in this case, the exaggeration is physical—and may reflect the zany psychological characteristics of the characters.

CARICATURE. This is a form of portraiture in which a character's likeness is preserved but great liberties are taken with his or her face (Figure 7.6). This technique is often used in political cartoons to ridicule a person. Often, the person portrayed is put into some embarrassing situation—usually of political or social significance and frequently unflattering in nature.

We should not underestimate the power of caricature. It is used by many political cartoonists, often with devastating results, as most newspaper editorial pages demonstrate.

MISTAKES. Here we find characters misunderstanding gestures or making other mistakes that have a visual dimension to them. This kind of humor may be described as humor of identity: it involves something problematic with identity, as in the case of a dog begging in front of a statue of a man who seems to be holding something to eat or a porcupine mistaking a cactus for another porcupine and saying to it, "I love you."

VISUAL PUNS. Here we take a linguistic pun and play with it and generate visual puns to go along with it. I have, for example, taken the word *con* (as in *convict*) and drawn a number of visual puns based on the term: content, concave, and so on. These puns use the cartoon convention of the convict as a person in striped clothing and sometimes chained to a huge iron ball as a point of departure (Figure 7.7).

COMIC ILLUSTRATIONS. With this technique, a drawing comments on or relates somehow (often quite indirectly) in a funny way to something in the text. The secret is to visualize a drawing or cartoon that people will connect with the content of the text.

HUMOROUS ALLUSIONS. Here the artist plays on certain historical, legendary, or mythological figures or events in the public's mind for comic effect, essentially by parodying them. Heroes and heroines from films, novels, or the comics can also be used. This technique is often used in political cartoons, where a politician is shown as a would-be Superman or a Greek god or some other figure, except that the drawing pokes fun at the person (who is also caricatured). In some cases, the cartoonists use "types" of persons or characters, such as Huns or wimps or zanies of one sort or another. There is an

140

▌ FIGURE 7.7
Arthur Asa Berger,
"CONS." These drawings
are visual puns that play
with sounds and mean-
ings. What are these
"cons"? See page 146 for
answers.

unflattering connection made (or comparison) between the figure and the type portrayed (Figure 7.8).

The cartoon, then, by utilizing our collective consciousness and various techniques of visual comedy, is a powerful and popular art form.

Animated Cartoons

The term *animation* has to do with giving life to something, with making something seem alive and active. Animation can be defined as the process of filming two-dimensional drawings or three-dimensional objects (such as puppets or clay figures) so as to produce the illusion of motion. Animated cartoons are drawings that originally were photographed on movie film to

▌ FIGURE 7.8
Cartoon images permeate
contemporary art. Here
they are used in a work of
electronic art—George
Legrady's *Slippery Traces*.

give the illusion that the characters drawn are alive and can move and talk.

The movie cameras used for making animated films have to be fitted with a device that allows single-frame action—that is, one frame to be shot at a time. With computers, of course, this is not necessary. (Computer animation that simulates real-life figures is discussed in Chapter 9.)

With 35-mm and 70-mm movie cameras, twenty-four frames are shot each second for sound film. This means that an artist must draw twenty-four pictures, each with a minimal increment of movement, to create the illusion of motion. If fewer than twenty-four pictures are drawn for a second's worth of film, the motion seems jerky. Winsor McKay, a comic strip artist, generally is credited with producing the first successful animated film—*Gertie, the Trained Dinosaur*—in 1909. In 1928, Walt Disney produced *Steamboat Willie*, which featured synchronous sound (sound effects that were synchronized with the visual images). With the release in 1937 of Disney's first feature, *Snow White and the Seven Dwarfs*, the age of animated feature-length films was upon us.

As noted previously, other methods of animation besides drawings created by artists or generated by computers are available. Another important animation technique is *claymation*, a form of object animation in which figures sculpted in clay are changed very slowly, with each change filmed, to give the illusion of motion. Clay figures typically are changed twenty-four times for a second's worth of animated film. Objects like dolls, puppets, animal figures, and the like can also be animated and, so to speak, brought to life.

If it takes 24 drawings to do one second of a typical animated film, that means it takes 1,440 frames to do one minute (60 times 24) and 86,400 frames to do an hour-long film. Obviously, prior to the development of computer animation programs, the amount of work needed to make animated films was enormous. Whole armies of artists were needed to make the earliest feature-length animated films; *Snow White,* for example, used some 400,000 drawings.

One shortcut that was used before computers was cel animation. Using clear plastic overlays known as *cels,* artists drew not completely new images for each shot, but only the parts of the images that moved—for example, a finger or facial expression. These cels are now quite valuable and are sold as works of art, at very high prices, in many art galleries.

Animation using cartoons or drawings—technically, two-dimensional animation—should not be regarded as an art form exclusively for children. Many artists have used animation to create powerful films dealing with political and social issues, often using humor or, in countries where there was repression and censorship, indirection. In fact, numerous festivals worldwide are held to present the best animated films.

Animators distinguish between character animation, which involves drawings of people and objects, and graphic animation, which involves material such as logos, graphics, and photographic stills. Animators also work for different media: some for broadcast media or home video, and others for disk-based media, such as CDs, floppy disks, interactive media, and so on. Each of these media has different requirements.

For example, character animation involves issues such as how characters walk and move, how they use their mouths to make sounds, and how they rearrange their features to express emotions. Usually, artists draw their characters on paper and scan the drawings and then use computers to set the characters in motion, mask them, and colorize them. In some cases, animators take film footage of characters doing certain things and then animate this footage by a process known as rotoscoping. Fractal's *Painter* is one of the most commonly used software packages for this kind of work, but there are many others. In Hollywood, many animators use high-end packages like *Amazon Paint, PowerAnimator, Pandemonium,* and *Liberty* that run on Silicon Graphics platforms.

In sum, animation is an important branch of the film medium. And the development of inexpensive computer animation software programs has opened up even greater possibilities for writers and artists who wish to take advantage of the unique properties of animation.

THE IMPACT OF COMICS AND CARTOONS

The elements in comic strips and cartoons may be relatively simple—line drawings and words, for the most part—but the impact of these art forms can be quite strong. We now recognize that seemingly simple phenomena can trigger powerful emotional responses in people, because these phenomena (the sound of rain, a symbol, a kind of lighting) often are connected to profoundly important experiences people have had, which are stored in their memories and called to mind, somehow, by something in the comic strip or cartoon—just as they are by verbal or visual images in "classic" literature or art.

The pictorial arts have a long history—from drawings on the walls of caves, thousands and thousands of years ago, to the latest episode of *Peanuts* or *Doonesbury* found in the morning newspaper. There is a kind of magic and power to capturing an image that we have recognized and made use of— for millennia, it would seem. Some scholars have suggested that precursors of the comic book appeared centuries ago, and we know that the political cartoon has been around for hundreds of years.

One reason the comic book and cartoon have been so popular is that they are extremely flexible and can be used for a variety of purposes. For example, the U.S. Army has found that it is helpful to use the comic book format in teaching soldiers how to use and maintain some equipment. And many people use a form of cartoon—greeting cards—to express emotions indirectly, especially emotions that they find it hard to communicate directly (Figure 7.9).

Comics and cartoons also can be used for advertising; the comic strip simulates action and has the power of the storyboard, which is used in designing commercials. From McLuhan's point of view, the storyboard, having less information than the commercial, would generate stronger involvement on the part of readers than would the commercial itself.

And we all have seen how the comic strip has evolved into the animated film, which is a remarkable medium that can generate very powerful experiences. The early animated films were simple and funny; but as animation has developed, it has led to what might be described as serious animated films that use the power of the artist to create incredible characters, scenes, and events. The animated film makes possible a style called "the fantastic" and expands our horizons immeasurably.

Finally, there is the matter of the power comic strips and cartoons have to generate humor (Figure 7.10). Humor is a great enigma; philosophers and scientists have been fascinated by it all through history, and many of our greatest minds, from Aristotle to Sigmund Freud, have tried to explain what humor is and what functions it has for people. Cartoons and comics usually generate a smile or two rather than laughter—but this smile is a signifier of

■ **Figure 7.9**
Chris Van Dusen, "Happy Birthday, Mom." Greeting cards like this help us express our emotions with less embarrassment.

■ **Figure 7.10**
Arthur Asa Berger, selections from "Nosology." Here the author plays with "noses" (and sounds related to them) to create a zany kind of quiz. The title spoofs the medical term *nosology*. What are these "noses"? Here are some hints. (A) He thinks noses may not exist. (B) This tells a tale of adventure in Africa. (C) He has a taste for blood. (D) He had a way with words, but women scorned him. See page 146 for answers.

some kind of a humorous message that has been received and understood. How this happens is still a considerable mystery. We know what techniques the cartoonists and comic strip artists and writers use, but we do not know why pictorial humor makes us laugh.

CONCLUSIONS

The fact that many comic strips and comic books are funny has led people to underestimate their significance, because people often assume that things that are funny (or not serious) do not have the same status as so-called serious works. We no longer make this mistake, and now many scholars and researchers are studying humor, in all of its manifestations, and granting it great importance. We have discovered that humor has important psychological, sociological, political, and even physiological significance. Humor stimulates the heart and produces various kinds of relaxation effects.

It is worth noting, then, that some of our greatest humorists are our comic strip artists and cartoonists. And, in the same vein, some of our most significant—in terms of their impact on the general public—creative artists have been our comic strip and comic book creators and our cartoonists.

APPLICATIONS

1. Assume you have been hired by a company that creates comic books. Create a comic book superhero or superheroine and draw the cover. How will you make your character different? Interesting? Use colors and make your drawing the size of comic books (seven by ten inches).

2. Create an origin tale, two pages long, for your character. (The origin tale of *Superman* is two pages long.) Be sure to use all the conventions of the comic book: frames, dialogue, action, and so on. Do you think you have created a compelling tale? Why or why not? Did you enjoy the process?

3. Make a content analysis of the comics page of your local newspaper. Do the following: count the number of frames, count the number of words spoken by male and female (and other) characters, count the number of times you see male and female figures, classify the strips in some manner, and list the topics discussed or alluded to. What do the comics (or, at least, the ones you've studied) reflect about American society and culture? Are any groups underrepresented? Or not represented at all?

4. Try drawing caricatures of your friends. You might find profiles are easiest, but you can try full face or three-quarter face if you wish. Try to

capture their likenesses and, at the same time, exaggerate their features. Does this exercise make you see them in a new light?

5. Using a mirror, try drawing full-face caricatures of yourself. Which features will you exaggerate? Does this exercise make you see yourself in a new light?

6. Using your skill as a caricaturist, try drawing a political cartoon. You can use the work of political cartoonists as models to imitate, but the idea for the cartoon should be your own. Does this exercise give you a better appreciation of these cartoonists?

ANSWERS:

"CONS"

(A) Second baseman

(B) Concave

(C) Content

(D) Condor

"Nosology"

(A) Agnosetic

(B) The Nose of Kilmanjaro

(C) Noseferatu (see page 96)

(D) Cyranose de Bergerac

TYPOGRAPHY AND GRAPHIC DESIGN:
Tools of Visual Communication

Every newspaper, book, and magazine we read has been designed by a graphic designer, who selects the typefaces these publications use. Every word we read reflects a choice by a typographer or designer. In a real sense, typography and graphic arts are the arts that impact most directly on the printed material we read in every medium and art form.

TYPOGRAPHY

Typography is, for our purposes, the art of selecting and arranging type or—in broader terms—using type in various graphic designs to obtain particular effects. Whenever you see any printed matter, the typefaces in which that material is set are based on someone's decision about which typefaces to use, how wide the margins should be, and so on. In the case of print advertisements, the decision is made by a specialist in type or, in some cases, by the art director in an agency.

Typefaces vary greatly—they have different looks and different meanings for people. Certain typefaces are very formal and elegant; others are casual and relaxed. Some typefaces suggest antiquity; others are very modern. The point is that, just as the size of the television screen affects television programs, so do the typefaces chosen affect how people will interpret a given message. The typeface is the medium and the words set into print are the message, to recall McLuhan's ideas. The evocative power of different typefaces is particularly important in advertising, though it also affects the way we react to books and periodicals.

Types, like all of printing, are tools in communication. Printing puts information into someone's hands, influences him to feel or think a certain way, or prompts him to take or refrain from taking a certain action. The typeface is the trigger part of that tool, so to speak, because it determines the way the message looks to the reader—pleasant, pretty, messy, painful or threatening—and this in turn affects the reader's reaction to the printed message.

–J. BEN LIEBERMAN,
TYPES OF TYPEFACES

Ever since Johannes Gutenberg developed movable type in 1440 and revolutionized communication by making books available to the masses (ultimately, when printing became widespread), typographers have been developing different typefaces and artists have been experimenting with graphic design.

TYPEFACES

We describe the size of type in *points* and *picas,* not inches. There are 12 points to a pica and approximately 6 picas to an inch. Thus, we talk about 10-point type or 12-point type. Then there is the matter of the design of the letters, which involves the following features:

Basic shape	Proportion of the parts
Stance (lean)	Weight or blackness
Dimensions	Contrast among parts
Size of letter	Contour or outline
Width of letter	Alignment along reading line
Quality of line	Kinds of strokes

Basic Classifications

In addition to these elements, there are many ways of classifying and describing typefaces (and there are, it is estimated, thousands of typefaces currently being used). Some of these classifications are discussed in the following sections.

TEXT VERSUS DISPLAY TYPEFACES. Text typefaces are designed to be easy to read and are used for text in books, magazines, newspapers, and other media. Display typefaces—found in titles, headings, and the like—are used to generate a graphic idea or attitude. They are very suggestive: they catch our attention and give personality to the messages they convey.

SERIF VERSUS SANS SERIF TYPEFACES. A serif is a short cross-line found at the ends of letters. Serifs originally were used in stone-cut Roman capital letters as a means of finishing off a stroke. There are variations in the size and shape of serifs, but serif faces are a general category. Some typographers believe that serif faces are easier to read than sans serif faces because serifs help tie the letters of a word together. This book is set in 10.5/12 Berkeley, a serif typeface.

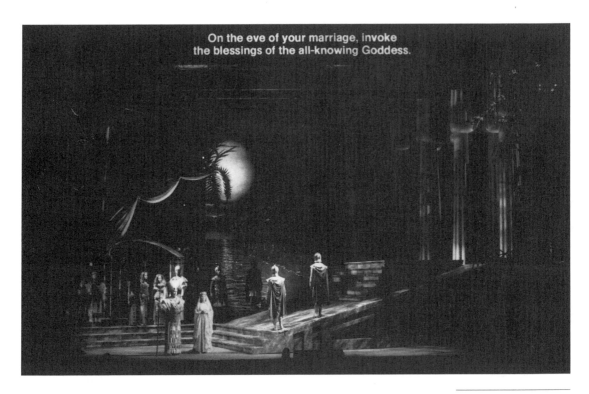

On the eve of your marriage, invoke
the blessings of the all-knowing Goddess.

FIGURE 8.1

Act II of Verdi's *Aida*, "The Banks of the Nile, Outside the Temple of Isis," as seen in the San Francisco Opera's 1984 Summer Season production. Note the supertitle, in a sans serif face, on the screen at the top of the photograph. The sans serif face was used because of its readability and because it also offers a contemporary look. These supertitles have revolutionized opera productions and made it possible for American audiences to know what is happening in operas in considerably more detail than before.

As the phrase suggests, *sans serif typefaces* lack serifs and have a cleaner, more contemporary look about them than serif typefaces. Figure 8.1 shows an example of a sans serif typeface.

OLD ENGLISH AND ROMAN TYPEFACES. *Old English typefaces* are similar to the one used by Gutenberg in printing his Bible. He developed it out of the manuscript letter style used by medieval scribes. It is beautiful but very difficult to read for long periods of time.

Roman typefaces were developed in the fifteenth century and were modeled after the writing styles of Roman scribes. These faces developed into three classes: Old Style, with somewhat rounded serifs and little variation in line thickness; Transitional, with more open letters and rounded serifs (such as **Baskerville**); and Modern, with more contrast between thick and thin lines and thin, straight serifs (such as **Bodoni**). Figure 8.2 gives examples of some typefaces, and Figure 8.3 shows characteristics of the different classes.

LIGHT, BOLD, AND ITALIC TYPEFACES. A given type family often comes in many different weights in terms of the thickness of the lines. Thus, we have bold

b

ITC Barcelona*
Book
Book Italic
Medium
Medium Italic
Bold
Bold Italic
Heavy
Heavy Italic

ITC Bauhaus*
Light
Medium
Demi
Bold

ITC Benguiat*
Book
Book Italic
Medium
Medium Italic
Bold
Bold Italic
Book Condensed
Book Condensed Italic
Medium Condensed
Medium Condensed Italic
Bold Condensed
Bold Condensed Italic

ITC Benguiat Gothic*
Book
Book Italic
Medium
Medium Italic
Bold
Bold Italic
Heavy
Heavy Italic

ITC Berkeley Oldstyle*
Book
Book Italic
Medium
Medium Italic
Bold
Bold Italic
Black
Black Italic

NEW FROM ITC

ITC Tiepolo™
Book
Book Italic
Bold
Bold Italic
Black
Black Italic

a

ITC American Typewriter*
Light
Medium
Bold
Light Condensed
Medium Condensed
Bold Condensed

ITC Avant Garde Gothic*
Extra Light
Extra Light Oblique
Book
Book Oblique
Medium
Medium Oblique
Demi
Demi Oblique
Bold
Bold Oblique
Book Condensed
Medium Condensed
Demi Condensed
Bold Condensed

b

ITC Bookman*
Light
Light Italic
Medium
Medium Italic
Demi
Demi Italic
Bold
Bold Italic

ITC Caslon No. 224*
Book
Book Italic
Medium
Medium Italic
Bold
Bold Italic
Black
Black Italic

ITC Century*
Light
Light Italic
Book
Book Italic
Bold
Bold Italic
Ultra
Ultra Italic
Light Condensed
Light Condensed Italic
Book Condensed
Book Condensed Italic
Bold Condensed
Bold Condensed Italic
Ultra Condensed
Ultra Condensed Italic

c

ITC Cheltenham*
Light
Light Italic
Book
Book Italic
Bold
Bold Italic
Ultra
Ultra Italic
Light Condensed
Light Condensed Italic
Book Condensed
Book Condensed Italic
Bold Condensed
Bold Condensed Italic
Ultra Condensed
Ultra Condensed Italic

ITC Clearface*
Regular
Regular Italic
Bold
Bold Italic
Heavy
Heavy Italic
Black
Black Italic

ITC Cushing*
Book
Book Italic
Medium
Medium Italic
Bold
Bold Italic
Heavy
Heavy Italic

ITC Élan™
Book
Book Italic
Medium
Medium Italic
Bold
Bold Italic
Black
Black Italic

e

ITC Eras*
Light
Book
Medium
Demi
Bold
Ultra

ITC Esprit™
Book
Book Italic
Medium
Medium Italic
Bold
Bold Italic
Black
Black Italic

ITC Fenice*
Light
Light Italic
Regular
Regular Italic
Bold
Bold Italic
Ultra
Ultra Italic

ITC Franklin Gothic*
Book
Book Italic
Medium
Medium Italic
Demi
Demi Italic
Heavy
Heavy Italic

Friz Quadrata
Friz Quadrata
Friz Quadrata Bold

ITC Galliard*
Roman
Roman Italic
Bold
Bold Italic
Black
Black Italic
Ultra
Ultra Italic

▌ Figure 8.2
Examples of typefaces.

Type categories	General characteristics						
1. Sloping e-Bar (Venetian Serif) Nos 1-34 e.g. **6** Kennerley, **19** Centaur, **30** ITC Souvenir, and **32** Italian Old Style (Monotype).	little contrast	e-bar sloped	angled or vertical stress	oblique ascender serif (not always)	foot serif often oblique (not always)	oblique lower case serif (not always)	**SLOPING E-BAR** (VENETIAN SERIF)
2. Angled Stress/Oblique Serifs (Old Style Serif) Nos 35-53 e.g. **35** Bembo, **39** Plantin, **44** Trump Mediaeval and **53** Times New Roman (Monotype).	medium contrast	e-bar horizontal	angled stress	oblique ascender serif	oblique foot serif	oblique lower case serif	**ANGLED STRESS OBLIQUE SERIFS** (OLD STYLE SERIF)
3. Vertical Stress/Oblique Serifs (Transitional Serif) Nos 54-110 e.g. **61** Caslon 540, **78** Baskerville 169 (Monotype), **92** Garamond (Stempel) and **105** Romulus.	good contrast	e-bar horizontal	stress vertical (or nearly so)	oblique serifs	foot serif usually level (not always)	oblique lower case serif	**VERTICAL STRESS OBLIQUE SERIFS** (TRANSITIONAL SERIF)
4. Vertical Stress/Straight Serifs (New Transitional Serif) e.g. **111** Joanna, **119** Century Schoolbook, **123** Cheltenham, and **138** Melior.	little contrast	e-bar horizontal	vertical stress	straight serifs (some slightly oblique)		straight serif in lower case (some oblique)	**VERTICAL STRESS STRAIGHT SERIFS** (NEW TRANSITIONAL)
5. Abrupt Contrast/Straight Serifs (Modern Serif) Nos 151-187 e.g. **153** Bauer Bodoni, **161** Walbaum (Linotype), **174** Caledonia and **185** Scotch Roman.	abrupt contrast	e-bar horizontal	vertical stress	line or bracketed serifs	straight serifs	straight serifs	**ABRUPT CONTRAST STRAIGHT SERIFS** (MODERN SERIF)
6. Slab Serif Nos 188-217 e.g. **197** Rockwell, **203** Schadow Antiqua, **209** Clarendon (Linotype), and **214** ITC American Typewriter.	little or no contrast	square slab serifs	single storey / double storey	bracketed serifs	single storey / double storey	rounded serif	**SLAB SERIF**
7. Wedge Serif (Hybrid Serif) Nos 218-240 e.g. **218** Albertus, **233** Meridien, **236** Copperplate Gothic and **240** Romic.	poor contrast	wedge-ended serifs	wedge-shaped serifs	fine line terminals	half serif only		**WEDGE SERIF** (HYBRID SERIF)
8. Sans Serif Nos 245-304 e.g. **254** Futura, **259** Gill Sans, **267** Univers 55 and **279** Helvetica.	little or no contrast	wide medium narrow (no spur)	wide medium narrow (spur)	special shape (rounded)			**SANS SERIF**

FIGURE 8.3
Basic characteristics of type.

faces, which are heavier and blacker than regular faces, and other faces that are lighter than regular faces.

Invented in 1501 by Aldus Manutius, italics are a slanted face, modeled after handwriting. Most typefaces have regular versions and italic ones, which are often used for emphasis. In scholarly writing, for example, we use italics to indicate the names of books and foreign words and phrases and to emphasize a word or passage in some text.

A BRIEF GLOSSARY ON TYPE

The following list briefly defines some key typographical terms discussed in this chapter, as well as some other important terms.

Ascenders. The segment of certain lowercase letters (b, d, f, h, k, l, and t) that extends above the height of a typical lowercase letter such as e or a.

Baseline. The imaginary line at the bottom of a line of type, on which the letters seem to rest.

Descenders. The part of certain lowercase letters (g, j, p, q, and y) that descend below the baseline.

Hairlines. The thin strokes at the end of letters in serif typefaces.

Justified left. Lines of type that are flush at the left-hand margin of the page.

Justified right. Lines of type that are flush at the right-hand margin of the page.

Justified. Lines of type that are justified at both the left-hand and right-hand margins of the page.

Kerning. Adjustment of a letter so that it sets in the space of another letter.

Letterspacing. Spaces added between letters in a line to improve the look of the line.

Ligature. Two characters (and sometimes more) linked together to form a single element. Common ligatures are fi and fl.

Pica. A standard typographical measure equivalent to 12 points. This term is derived from an old printer's term for type that was 12 points.

Point. A standard typographical measure equivalent to approximately 1/72 inch. Twelve points make one pica.

Ragged. Type that has an irregular line on one or both margins. If the type is unjustified on the left, it is "ragged left"; if the type is unjustified on the right, it is "ragged right."

Sans serif. Typefaces that do not have lines crossing the main strokes or elements of a given character. Some common sans serif typefaces are **Futura** and **Helvetica.**

Serif. Typefaces that have lines crossing the main strokes of a given character. Serifs vary: they can be square or oblique, thick or thin.

Typeface family. A group of typefaces that are variations on a common design. The common variations are roman, bold, italic, condensed (the letters are narrow), and extended (the letters are broad).

Weight. The "heaviness" of a typeface. If the strokes in the letters in a typeface are thick, the typeface is "heavyweight"; if they are thin, the typeface is "lightweight."

CAPITAL VERSUS LOWERCASE LETTERS. The capital (uppercase) is generally larger and taller than the lowercase letter and is used at the beginnings of sentences and for titles, proper nouns, and display purposes. It is difficult to read long passages of material set in uppercase.

Lowercase letters have a different design from capital letters and are not just smaller capital letters. Lowercase letters have ascenders and descenders that give variety and facilitate distinguishing between letters.

To see the difference between reading something entirely in capitals and reading something in capitals and lowercase type, look at the following example:

WE THE PEOPLE OF THE UNITED STATES, IN ORDER TO FORM A MORE PERFECT UNION, ESTABLISH JUSTICE, INSURE DOMESTIC TRANQUILITY, PROVIDE FOR THE COMMON DEFENCE, PROMOTE THE GENERAL WEL-FARE, AND SECURE THE BLESSINGS OF LIBERTY TO OURSELVES AND OUR POSTERITY, DO ORDAIN AND ESTABLISH THIS CONSTITUTION FOR THE UNITED STATES OF AMERICA.

We the People of the United States, in Order to form a more perfect Union, establish Justice, insure domestic Tranquility, provide for the common defence, promote the general Welfare, and secure the Blessings of Liberty to ourselves and our Posterity, do ordain and establish this CONSTITUTION for the United States of America.

Obviously, the second passage is much easier to read than the first passage. There is more white space around the letters in the second passage, which seems to facilitate comprehension.

Readability is not always a function of the size of the type. We can see that the passage done in capitals has larger type but is more difficult to read. Readability is connected to the way the combination of letters creates a quickly perceived word image.

POINTS. Type sizes were, at one time, identified by name, but this convention has given way to identifying them by points. (The point system was developed in France in 1737 by Pierre Simon Fournier.) A point is about 1/72 inch. Twelve points are known as a pica. When describing the size of type, we use points and thus might talk about 12-point type or 18-point type. Figure 8.4 shows examples of type size.

CONDENSED AND EXPANDED TYPEFACES. Some typefaces have very narrow letters and are known as condensed faces. These faces allow one to print more text in a given area than if one uses regular faces. There are also expanded faces, which feature very wide letters and use more space than regular faces and much more space than condensed faces.

As this brief introduction to typography suggests, typefaces play an important role in transmitting information, and the way a message is presented has a great deal of significance. Typography is a highly skilled art and plays an important role in shaping the way people respond to printed matter. Typographers often say that typography should be "invisible" and should not be noticed by the reader; that is, it should not call attention to itself because

SABON

ROMAN

Excellence in typography is the result of nothing more than an attitude. Its appeal comes from the understanding used in its planning; the designer must care. In contemporary advertising the perfect integration of design elements often demands unorthodox typography. It may require the use of compact spacing, minus leading, unusual sizes and weights; whatever is needed to improve appearance and impact. Stating specific principles or guides on the subject of typography is difficult because the principle applying to

7 POINT

Excellence in typography is the result of nothing more than an attitude. Its appeal comes from the understanding used in its planning; the designer must care. In contemporary advertising the perfect integration of design elements often demands unorthodox typography. It may require the use of compact spacing, minus leading, unusual sizes

9 POINT

BOLD

Excellence in typography is the result of nothing more than an attitude. Its appeal comes from the understanding used in its planning; the designer must care. In contemporary advertising the perfect integration of design elements often demands unorthodox typography. It may require the use of compact spacing, minus leading, unusual sizes and weights; whatever is needed to improve appearance and impact. Stating specific principles or guides on the subject of typography is difficult because the principle applying to

Excellence in typography is the result of nothing more than an attitude. Its appeal comes from the understanding used in its planning; the designer must care. In contemporary advertising the perfect integration of design elements often demands unorthodox typography. It may require the use of compact spacing, minus leading, unusual sizes

ITALIC

Excellence in typography is the result of nothing more than an attitude. Its appeal comes from the understanding used in its planning; the designer must care. In contemporary advertising the perfect integration of design elements often demands unorthodox typography. It may require the use of compact spacing, minus leading, unusual sizes and weights; whatever is needed to improve appearance and impact. Stating specific principles or guides on the subject of typography is difficult because the principle applying to one job may not fit the next. No two jobs are identical

7 POINT

Excellence in typography is the result of nothing more than an attitude. Its appeal comes from the understanding used in its planning; the designer must care. In contemporary advertising the perfect integration of design elements often demands unorthodox typography. It may require the use of compact spacing, minus leading, unusual sizes

9 POINT

BOLD ITALIC

Excellence in typography is the result of nothing more than an attitude. Its appeal comes from the understanding used in its planning; the designer must care. In contemporary advertising the perfect integration of design elements often demands unorthodox typography. It may require the use of compact spacing, minus leading, unusual sizes and weights; whatever is needed to improve appearance and impact. Stating specific principles or guides on the subject of typography is difficult because the principle applying to one job may not fit the next. No

Excellence in typography is the result of nothing more than an attitude. Its appeal comes from the understanding used in its planning; the designer must care. In contemporary advertising the perfect integration of design elements often demands unorthodox typography. It may require the use of compact spacing, minus leading, unusual sizes the purpose of printing is to produce material that is read. In such cases, it is all the more powerful.

Maximizing the Impact of Type

Let's review some of the considerations to keep in mind when laying out a print advertisement, a newsletter, or anything that has a visual/textual dimension to it.

TYPEFACE. We have already seen that the choice of typeface is important, because different typefaces have distinctive personalities. Each typeface is a means of managing impressions in the minds of readers. And the typeface must be coordinated with any drawings or photographs being used in the visual field. In the case of advertisements or other kinds of promotional literature, for example, the typefaces must fit with the product "image" that is to be created or reinforced (Figure 8.5).

◀ FIGURE 8.4

Examples of typeface sizes and font variations within one type family. Not only are there many typefaces, but each typeface comes in many styles and different sizes.

▌ FIGURE 8.5

Type not only creates words, but can be used to create an image such as this flask, which is typical of those found in scientific laboratories.

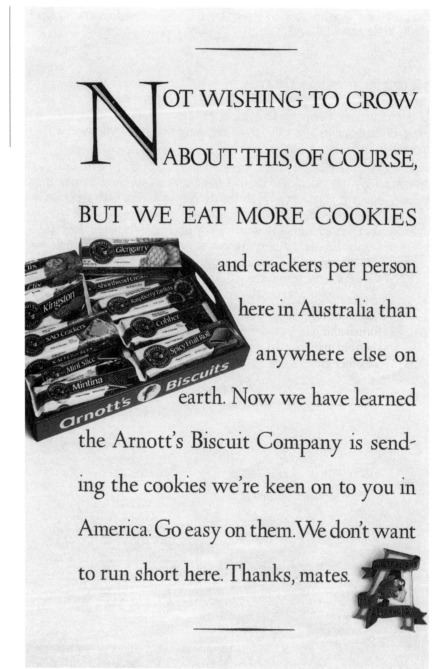

TYPE SIZE. We are also affected by the size of a given typeface, because size affects the way we respond to the design of individual letters.

LEADING. The amount of white space between the lines of print is referred to as *leading*. We respond, unconsciously, to extremely minute changes in the amount of leading, because the leading can give printed material a light and open look or, conversely, a heavy, dense look (Figure 8.6).

LETTERSPACING. Here, too, small differences have major consequences. This holds true especially for display type, where the letters are relatively large and the eye can see when letters are too close to one another, or the reverse. Experts pay great attention to these things. Although they may seem trivial, if you think of the design of an advertisement, newsletter, brochure, magazine, or other publication as a means of shaping people's perceptions, small things add up to big differences in effectiveness and impact.

MARGINS. In recent years, the notion of having ragged-right margins (that is, margins that do not line up) has become popular. The ragged-right margin conveys a different feeling than a flush-right (or justified) margin does—it has a less formal and, some would say, more contemporary feel to it. The size of top and bottom margins and the way text is placed relative to photographs, drawings, or other graphic material also affects the final image.

CHECKLIST ON TYPOGRAPHY

The following checklist focuses on various aspects of typography to keep in mind when preparing or analyzing documents of any kind. Above all, adhere to these three basic rules: keep it simple; make things easy for the reader; and, when in doubt, throw it out.

1. Are too many typefaces used, causing clutter and distracting readers?
2. Are the lines of type too long, making them hard to read?
3. Do elements such as photographs and graphics not line up, thereby distracting readers?
4. Is the type in titles and headings too large, making pages top-heavy?
5. Is the page overcrowded with material, diminishing its emphasis and readability?
6. Is the typeface too heavy, too condensed, or too large, making it hard to read?
7. Is there insufficient contrast between the type and the background, reducing readability?
8. Is there insufficient space (or leading) between lines, making them hard to read?

❚ FIGURE 8.7

This handsome envelope is full of beautiful stamps from Spain. Post offices in many countries nowadays prefer to print the amount of money needed for mail that is being sent abroad on a plain piece of gummed paper with a characterless dot matrix printer. But it is still possible, with a bit of effort, to purchase all kinds of attractive stamps.

DESIGN. This term refers to how the different elements in a visual field are placed in relation to one another. Artists and designers have different sensibilities (as, in the case of advertising, do clients, who sometimes affect the outcome), which is why a group of six art directors would each turn out different-looking advertisements, even if given the same elements to work with: a photograph and text set into type. Even something as humble as an envelope with stamps, if they are interesting and if the "image" is artfully composed, can have a very pleasing aesthetic impact (Figure 8.7).

GENERAL PRINCIPLES OF DESIGN

The material we've discussed so far has applied to visual fields in general—that is, all of the visual arts—and in this chapter to specific kinds of visual materials—advertisements, brochures, manuals, magazines, and so on. The specific topics we've mentioned can be subsumed under some more general principles of design, many of which have been discussed or alluded to previously. They are brought together here.

Balance

Balance refers to the way basic elements in a design relate to one another. We discussed axial or formal balance and its opposite, dynamic or informal balance, in Chapter 3. Each generates a different kind of response. In general,

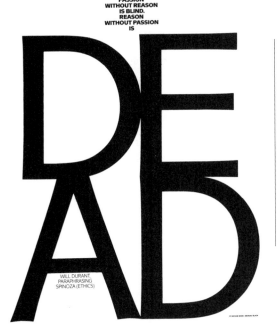

PASSION
WITHOUT REASON
IS BLIND.
REASON
WITHOUT PASSION
IS

DEAD

WILL DURANT,
PARAPHRASING
SPINOZA (ETHICS)

we must put the elements in a design into some kind of relationship that is visually effective and that accomplishes the mission of the work. Elements have different weights, depending on such things as size, shape, and color; and these weights must be tied together in some way to generate a visually functional balance.

Proportion

Here we are dealing with the size of different elements in a design. Recall from Chapter 3 that if balance involves the way elements relate to one another around imaginary vertical and horizontal axes, *proportion* involves how they relate to one another in general, relative to the size or area of the visual field being utilized—that is, the size of the advertisement, brochure, maga- zine, or whatever (Figure 8.8).

Let us take the example of a magazine cover. The size of the title is of some consequence. If it is too large and the typeface is too heavy (that is, out of proportion), the cover seems top-heavy and is disturbing. We all have a sense of correct proportions; when visual phenomena violate these notions or codes, we are bothered. Sometimes, of course, codes are violated on pur- pose, to achieve a particular effect. Tastes are continually changing when it comes to design, and what seems beautiful and tasteful and exciting one year can seem dull and banal a few years later.

Movement

Movement refers to the way elements in a composition lead our eyes along and force them to scan the composition for information. This movement (described by Zettl as involving what he calls "vectors") is accomplished by various means, such as line and shape and color. We know that the eye tends to favor the upper left corner in any visual field; it can then be drawn to various parts of the field by shapes and lines and other design elements.

Even when we look at a sculpture or a simple design, the eye scans in interesting ways. We tend to trace over the outline of a visual and follow lines and shapes that are presented to us by artists and designers. The fact that we seek movement and that visual phenomena can generate visual excitement and more or less "force" our eyes to move in certain directions is of considerable use not only to advertisers but to all visual artists.

Contrast

Previously, it was suggested that concepts have no meaning in themselves but only in relation to other concepts—with opposition being the most important relationship. The same applies to visual phenomena. It is through *contrasts*—differences in size, shape, color, and so on—that elements in a visual field acquire meaning. We know, for example, that a square of red looks different with a gray background than with an orange background. The figure is affected by the ground.

In some cases, when we wish elements to stand out, we emphasize contrast and thus have something simple standing against or placed in opposition to something busy, or something dark placed against something light. Contrasts generate attention. The power of color contrasts was used by pop and op artists to generate certain effects. Very strong colors and bright color contrasts also have certain class implications or associations and thus must be used with care. For example, walls that are painted bright colors tend to be avoided by upscale types, who paint their walls off-white as a rule.

Unity

Unity refers to the way all the elements in a composition or visual field relate to one another and produce a sense of completeness and wholeness. Related to unity is a *Gestalt effect,* a psychological and aesthetic response that is greater than the sum of its parts. In other words, the entire image may produce a response that is greater than would be produced by adding the various elements in the visual field. The opposite of unity is fragmentation, which suggests that the elements in the composition don't relate to one another, producing a sense that the work is incomplete.

In some cases, artists don't wish to generate a unified effect and so purposely use fragmentation to achieve a particular effect. *There are no absolute rules in design and composition, and the best designers and artists often violate rules.* In thinking about design, one should first consider the effect desired and then work to achieve that effect, using whatever techniques are available. So we work backwards, from the desired effect to whatever can be done to generate that effect.

DESIGN EXAMPLES

Two Versions of a Page

To show how changes in typography and design can give a publication a different look, consider Figures 8.9 and 8.10. It shows two "pages" that use the same copy but are worlds apart in terms of the way they look. Examine the typography and design in Figures 8.11, 8.12, and 8.13 in terms of the following considerations, which differentiate the two pages:

1. The right margins for the text
2. The use of display faces
3. The weight of the italics and their visibility
4. The size of the side margins and the location of text on the page relative to the margins
5. The margins on the top and bottom of the page
6. The lightness or heaviness of the text face
7. The size of the text face
8. The spacing between lines in the text face

The Talmud

The Talmud is a compendium of the oral law of the Jews, gathered together many hundreds of years ago and subject to the scrutiny and analysis of numerous rabbis and scholars. The typography of the Talmud is very interesting because different typefaces were used to represent the ideas of the most important commentators. On a given page of the Talmud, one might find four or five typefaces, snaking up and down the page, each reflecting an

■ FIGURE 8.9
Here is a poorly designed page. What's wrong with it? Why doesn't it work?

SEEING IS BELIEVING 103

an important role in transmitting information and that the way a message is presented has a great deal of significance. Typography is a highly skilled art and plays an important role in shaping the way people respond to printed matter. Typographers often say that typography should be "invisible" and should not be noticed by the reader.

DESIGNING THE VISUAL FIELD

Let me list some of the considerations to be kept in mind when laying out a print advertisement, a newsletter, or anything that has a visual dimension.

A. The Typeface

It has already been suggested that the choice of typefaces is important, since different typefaces have distinctive personalities. Each typeface is a means of managing impressions in the minds of readers. And the typeface must be coordinated with any drawings or photographs being used in the visual field. In the case of advertisements, for example, the typefaces must fit with the "image" of the product that is to be created or reinforced.

Artists and designers have different sensibilities (and in the case of advertising, so do clients) who sometimes affect things, which is why a group of six art directors would each turn out different looking advertisements, even if given the same elements to work with.[1]

B. The Size of the Face

We are also affected by the size of a given typeface, since size affects the way we respond to the design of individual letters.

The material discussed to this point was applied to visual fields in general and to specific kinds of visual materials—advertisements, brochures, manuals, magazines, etc. The topics mentioned can be subsumed under some more general principles of design, many of which have been mentioned or alluded to in various places in this book.

[1] Op cit. Berger, p. 123

an important role in transmitting information and that the way a message is presented has a great deal of significance. Typography is a highly skilled art and plays an important role in shaping the way people respond to printed matter. Typographers often say that typography should be "invisible" and should not be noticed by the reader.

DESIGNING THE VISUAL FIELD

Let me list some of the considerations to be kept in mind when laying out a print advertisement, a newsletter, or anything that has a visual dimension.

A. The Typeface It has already been suggested that the choice of typefaces is important, since different typefaces have distinctive personalities. Each typeface is a means of managing impressions in the minds of readers. And the typeface must be coordinated with any drawings or photographs being used in the visual field. In the case of advertisements, for example, the typefaces must fit with the "image" of the product that is to be created or reinforced.

> *Artists and designers have different sensibilities (and in the case of advertising, so do clients) who sometimes affect things, which is why a group of six art directors would each turn out different looking advertisements, even if given the same elements to work with.[1]*

B. The Size of the Face We are also affected by the size of a given typeface, since size affects the way we respond to the design of individual letters.

The material discussed to this point was applied to visual fields in general and to specific kinds of visual materials—advertisements, brochures, manuals, magazines, etc. The topics mentioned can be subsumed under some more general principles of design, many of which have been mentioned or alluded to in various places in this book.

---

[1] Op cit. Berger, p. 123

■ FIGURE 8.11

Front pages of selected newspapers. Look at *The Wall Street Journal* issue of April 29, 1997 (this page). This is an excellent example of typographic unity. The headlines, subheads, and textual matter are all relatively similar in size, and the illustrations are all small. This page projects an image of sobriety and high seriousness.

THE WALL STREET JOURNAL.

© 1997 Dow Jones & Company, Inc. All Rights Reserved.

XXXVI NO. 83   WE/PA   ★★★   TUESDAY, APRIL 29, 1997   INTERNET ADDRESS: http://wsj.com   · · ·   75 CENTS

■ FIGURE 8.12

Contrast Figure 8.11 with the front pages from the *Detroit Free Press* issue of October 7, 1996, and the *USA Today* issue of June 6–8, 1997 on the following page. These latter two papers have much different personalities, which are reflected on their front pages.

opinion on the main topic of the page, which was always printed in the largest and heaviest typeface. A typical page from the Talmud is shown in Figure 8.14.

The main section is in heavy type and looks like an inverted **T**. Then, above and below it, in different typefaces, are commentaries by some of its classic interpreters. The Talmud runs to many, many volumes and is a work of extraordinary complexity and intellectual sophistication, full of astounding feats of logical deduction and brilliant insights into the human condition. It is impossible to give here more than a brief sense of what it is like or of the incredible number of interpretations of ideas and events that are to be found in it.

This use of different typefaces to suggest different views is not limited to the Talmud. The page from a business magazine shown in Figure 8.15 also employs different faces to suggest different ideas and points of view. Note also, on this page, the exaggerated size of the quote marks and the way the typographer used ragged right for the body type and ragged left for the quoted material in the margins.

Many of the elements discussed previously, such as the use of white space, formal and informal balance, and contrast, go into the design of a book, magazine, or advertisement. There are also the aesthetic sensibilities of the audience to consider: certain designs that may appeal to "upscale" people will not appeal to "downscale" people—and artists, designers, and creative directors must always make certain that what they do will be appropriate for their audience.

DESIGN AND CONTROL

The pages we have just examined reflect something that we seldom think about—namely, that design has, in a sense, the power to control people and to evoke certain responses. The size of print, the style of print, the heaviness or lightness of print, the size of margins, the arrangement of the block of type on the page—these and countless other seemingly minor matters have a profound impact on how we respond to printed matter and visual phenomena in general (Figure 8.16). When we are browsing through a magazine, do we just glance at an advertisement and then turn the page, or do we pause for a moment to examine it? And if we do pause, what do we look at first? What do we read first?

These matters are of great concern to advertisers, who spend enormous amounts of money on their campaigns. It may be true that you can't tell a book by its cover, but experience tells us you can *sell* a book by its cover.

■ FIGURE 8.14

Page from the Talmud, showing different type-faces that are identified with different commentators. This shows the power of a typeface to confer an identity on someone or some institution.

changes its management system, we will see more powerful American competitors.

Akio Morita, Chairman of Sony, put the problem most succinctly:

The problem in the United States is management. Instead of meeting the challenge of a changing world, American business today is making small, short-term adjustments by cutting costs, by turning to the government for temporary relief.Success in trade is the result of patience and meticulous preparations with a long period of marketing preparation before the rewards are available.

The key to the future lies in how our businesses are managed. Much is being studied, written, and discussed about the changes that are necessary, but too little attention is paid to the personal qualities of managerial leadership and to the dimensions missing in many of today's managers.

Missing Dimensions

While I believe in the usefulness of management science and management systems, of long-range and strategic planning, the challenges we face will not be solved by more and better systems and techniques. While there is need to continue to push the frontiers of knowledge and enhance the contributions of management science, we must not forget that much of management is still art. Effective management is a combination of knowledge and intuition, of position and personality, of environmental constraints and human will, of time and chance.

There is no single theory of management sufficient in scope to guide intelligent action; nonetheless, there are rich conceptual resources that can guide the work of management. We can identify, for example, the qualities that distinguish excellence from mediocrity in managers. The critical dimensions lie, in my judgment, in the ability to orchestrate human talent and to bring the qualitative as well as the quantitative to bear effectively on the solution of complex problems. **David Lilienthal**, founder of the Tennessee Valley Administration and former chairman of the Atomic Energy Commission, expressed the idea this way:

The art of management is a high form of leadership, for it seeks to combine the act—the getting something done—with the meaning behind the act.

What makes management an artistic activity? For one, effective managers are required to integrate different and conflicting theories and themes. For another, effective managers must be able to engage issues on the level of both fact and feeling, to address questions that lie in the area of overlap between science and philosophy—between the tangible and the intangible. And finally, effective managers must overcome a lack of adequate theory to assist them in integrating talent, task, values, and technology.

Viewing management as an art form does not imply any lack of regard for scientific knowledge. One cannot ignore the impressive base of scholarship in management, in decision theory, in organizational theory. But today there are too few philosophers and too many managerial mechanics—enraptured with technique, never asking questions of meaning and purpose—captives to the bottom line of quarterly earnings without a vision or set of values to guide them. There are too few statesmen. There are too many technicians clothed in power and status, but lacking in heart, mind, and spirit.

How we identify, train, and nourish individuals with the qualities for managerial leadership is the challenge faced by management practitioners and scholars. Given such leaders, our ability to address our economic future is secure. The stakes are large, and the effort imperative.

Increasingly, we must come to face the challenges confronting us with the forthrightness, intelligence, creativity and pragmatism which historically have been the hallmarks of our private enterprise system. I believe that we are beginning to engage in the kind of critical self-appraisal and analysis that can ultimately provide the necessary foundations for New Management and, ultimately, for a national renaissance. I am pleased that this new publication is dedicated to helping managers undertake these crucial changes. For if we continue this process, America can emerge from this period—reinforced and reinvigorated by the experience—with our economy, our society, and our values intact for generations to come.

"Absence of adequate tax incentives for capital investment, obsolete plant and equipment, insufficient research and development, the decline of the work ethic, poor labor relations, and problems with government all contribute to the problem. But in my judgment, management inadequacy is by far the greatest single cause."

"Much is being studied, written, and discussed about the changes that are necessary, but too little attention is paid to the personal qualities of managerial leadership and to the dimensions missing in many of today's managers."

5

I FIGURE 8.15
Page from *New Management*. Notice the similarity of this page and the Talmud in terms of use of different typefaces, representing different ideas on a single page.

■ FIGURE 8.16

Communiqué. The newsletter is a very powerful means of communication; it is flexible, inexpensive, and easy to produce. And when well designed, its impact is considerably enhanced.

Gannett Center for Media Studies

Communiqué

January 1987

Center makes west coast debut

For one day this month the Gannett Center will "move" to California.

On Jan. 26 the Center will present a special public panel discussion titled "Iran and Watergate: For the Media, the Lessons Learned" at the Mark Hopkins Hotel in San Fransisco.

The event, the Center's inaugural program on the west coast, will be held in conjunction with a meeting of the Center's National Advisory Committee and will bring together many of the west's most prominent media professionals and scholars.

National Advisory Committee Chairman Frank H.T. Rhodes and Gannett Center Executive Director Everette Dennis will introduce the Center and its programs, then present the panelists.

Among them will be at least three members of the National Advisory Committee—former *New York Times* reporter Nancy Hicks Maynard, ABC's Ann Compton, and former *Boston Globe* editor Tom Winship. Gannett Center Senior Fellow Burton Benjamin will also be on the panel, and Oakland *Tribune* publisher Bob Maynard and NAC member Michael Sovern, Columbia's president, are tentatively scheduled to participate on the panel also.

Several west coast Associates of the Gannett Center will also attend the program. The Center's Associates Program brings together leaders of many American institutions who bring their special experience and insights to the Center's programs.

Media Message People,
the new Gannett Center poster,
is free upon request. See p.6.

New fellows bring complementary interests

Five new fellows begin work at the Center in January, examining different aspects of important and interrelated issues, among them the professionalization of journalists and the economic changes affecting newspapers.

The new arrivals are: Ellis Cose, from the University of California at Berkeley; Jeff Greenfield of ABC News; Lawrence McGill of Northwestern University; John Merrill, from Louisiana State University; and Susan Tifft of *Time* magazine.

All five will be in residence at the Center through the spring.

Jeff Greenfield, whose appointment as a fellow was announced in November, will be studying "Media Handling of Unanticipated Domestic Political Crises."

New Senior Fellow John Merrill will be spending a good portion of his time in New York at the United Nations, studying the key people who cover the U.N. for foreign papers and the role of their coverage in forming international

diplomatic opinion. While many studies have looked at the role of American journalists in this process, foreign journalists have been largely ignored.

Ellis Cose's study will also examine a select group of journalists—future ones. "There are interesting leadership changes going on," Cose says, "a changing of the guard in the editorial and business sense. Newspaper companies in the future will be substantially different, and my project is an inquiry into where present and future leaders are trying to take us and their companies."

Looking at the changes in the newspaper business from a different angle, Susan Tifft's project examines "The Coming of a New Economic Order to Media Ownership," a project she developed at least in part by looking at the old economic order: family ownership.

While at the Center, Tifft will also be working on a biography of the Bingham family, the former owners of the Louisville *Courier-Journal.*

Like Cose, new Research Fellow Larry McGill will be examining the way journalists come to positions of leadership, but McGill will focus on the role that particular news beats play in determining whether they get there.

"I once heard someone say that 85 percent of editors come from the political beat," McGill said, "and, as a sociologist, when I hear a precise number like that it sets off bells: Is it true? What values do top news people bring to their jobs? Where do they get them and how do they implement them?"

The new fellows join six others who are continuing fellowships at the Center— Burton Benjamin, Jerrold Footlick, Dan Schiller, Susan Shapiro, Sally Bedell Smith and Michael Moss—and come just as four others have returned to their professional and academic posts. David Anderson has returned to the University of Texas, Herbert Gans and Eleanor Singer have resumed their duties at Columbia, and Chris Ogan is back at Indiana University.

A Gannett Foundation Program at Columbia University

SUPERGRAPHICS

Supergraphics reflect an interesting phenomena: that a change in scale leads to a change in identity. Just as comic strip frames became works of art when they were blown up, painted in oils, put into a frame, and purchased by museums and art collectors, so does a word—that is, a group of letters—become an art object, so to speak, when it is enlarged into a *supergraphic.* The aesthetic components of each letter, which tend to be neglected when the letter is seen normal size, suddenly become visible.

In addition, the spaces and shapes created by huge letters are visually interesting and exciting. With supergraphics, then, we move from the printed page, where the mass of letters has an impact, to the gigantic wall, where a few letters or words and images, blown up to a great size, have an impact.

POSTMODERN DESIGN

In recent years, postmodernism has had an impact on newspaper and magazine design. *Postmodernism* (which means, literally, "after modernism") in design involves putting different styles together—as in Michael Graves' celebrated Portland building and a number of others like it—and essentially is ironic as well as eclectic. Kevin G. Barnhurst discusses the impact of postmodernism in *Seeing the Newspaper* (1994:196):

> In the 1980s, the postmodern style invaded graphic design from its origins in art and architecture. Postmodernism ransacks history, combining disparate stylistic effects with a mix of nostalgia and irony. It is a conservative movement that concentrates on illusion and surface effects. *USA Today,* which began publishing in 1982, incorporates the devices of Victorian newspapers, including narrow columns, varied headlines, vertical makeup, column rules, and a smaller scale overall. These are employed not in the mode of Victorian content but ironically for short snippets of text with amusing graphics and many pictures, in the mode of fast food, sound bites, and rock videos. Although other newspapers anticipated its use of graphics and color, *USA Today* has become a bellwether, marking the beginning of a new stylistic period.

This postmodern style of playfulness, pastiche, and stylistic eclecticism can also be found in magazines like *Wired, Mondo 2000,* and *Emigre.* In these magazines, the old design verities of simplicity, unity, and balance have been discarded. Postmodern design, in a less obvious manner, also has had an impact on many other general circulation magazines and, so some theorists argue, on American culture and society.

For example, postmodernists generally suggest that music videos and certain films, like *Blade Runner,* are postmodern in that they "quote" (imitate) conventions from other art forms, mix genres together, and reflect a much different sensibility than other kinds of films or videos. Music videos also tend to reject linear narratives, with beginnings, middles, and endings. This is important because we use (or perhaps, more correctly, we used to use) narratives to help us understand ourselves, to help us create meaning, to give us insights, and to help us situate ourselves in the chaotic world in which we live. When we reject logically structured narratives, we also reject the possibility of some kind of rational, coherent understanding of life. All we have, according to postmodernist theory, when pushed to its logical extremes, is images and snippets of this and that, occurring more or less at random.

Postmodernism was based on the rejection of modernism and offered us something different; now, some philosophers tell us, we are moving into a post-postmodern era. What impact this will have on television, films, videos, newspapers, magazines, and graphic design in general remains to be seen.

CONCLUSIONS

Some scholars believe that there are certain social, psychological, and political imperatives that flow from the development of movable type and printing. Printing, they suggest, leads to the development of a linear mode of thinking (generated by the lines of type we become used to reading) and, indirectly, to individualism and nationalism.

We need not go into such ramifications here; this brief investigation of a very complicated topic is meant to alert you to the power of type and typography, which, in combination with the photographic image (in its various manifestations) and the drawn or painted image, dominate our media and our visual experience.

APPLICATIONS

1. Duplicate four pages of text from various books. How do the different typefaces used in them generate different feelings? Consider such matters as type size, leading, weight, margin size, kind of margin (justified right or ragged right), and so on. Use this book as one of the four.

2. Write a short historical essay on a typeface that you like. Where did the typeface originate? How has it evolved? What features of the typeface appeal to you?

3. Find an example of typography that you think is particularly bad. Why is it bad?

4. Find an example of typography that you think is particularly good. Why is it good?

5. Assume a millionaire has given you a great deal of money and told you to create a new magazine. Decide on a subject matter, and choose a title. Then lay out the cover for the first issue. Using printed matter from other magazines whose style you like, dummy in a few pages to give a sense of the "look" of the magazine. What look were you striving for? Do you think you succeeded?

6. Find an image that you like, and analyze it according to the principles of design described in this chapter: balance, proportion, movement, contrast, and unity. Then do the same thing with an image that you don't like (which doesn't "work"). Why does one work but not the other?

7. Take photographs of any supergraphics in your living area, and analyze them using the criteria described in this chapter. If you were asked to design supergraphics for the same space, what would you do differently?

8. What do you think of the notion that the linearity of print has affected society? Will electronic media change things?

COMPUTERS AND GRAPHICS:
Wonders from the Image-Maker

Computers have had an enormous impact on all the arts—from desktop publishing to film. Now, with the development of the Internet, just about anyone with a computer and a modem can become a "published" writer and artist.

THE NATURE OF THE COMPUTER

Many people have the wrong idea about computers. Computers are electronic machines that can perform manipulations and calculations at incredible speeds, with data, using a program or stored set of instructions. Nevertheless, though computers are capable of incredibly fast operations with numbers, it is better to think of computers as devices that manipulate symbols or visual data rather than as adding machines or calculators. The most important symbol the computer can manipulate, as far as graphics are concerned, is the *pixel* (short for "picture element" or, in essence, a dot), which can be used to create lines, shapes, and other visual phenomena.

As Joseph Deken writes in *Computer Images: State of the Art* (1983:9):

> The versatility of computer images derives from the active electronic memory and processing systems that support them. While the computer memory-medium can store a direct literal representation of a single image, it can also generate an infinite variety of scenes from an internal computational model.

For capturing new images, the computer is an instrument of unparalleled reach. Entirely new worlds suddenly come into view: the thermal tides of the human body and the activity of the brain, for example; the geological and biological patterns of the earth's surface; or the radio-wave signatures of objects in space. Like the historic invention of the microscope and telescope, the development of computer-image processing has expanded our vision far beyond the range of the unaided human senses.

–JOSEPH DEKEN,
COMPUTER
IMAGES:
STATE OF THE ART

These computer images, he explains, offer "an entirely new form of visual communication, one that permits the individual viewer to adapt to and interact with the image itself" (1983:9).

The secret of the computer's image-making power lies in its ability to store pixels, or individual picture elements, and manipulate them. The computer image is a mosaic of pixels, arranged in rows and columns similar to the tiles in a mosaic. Each of these pixels is assigned a location and a predetermined color by the computer, which puts this information into memory and can call it up and manipulate it in innumerable ways, if it is being controlled by the right software.

Software programmers have developed many ingenious products in recent years, and many of the things that used to be done on mainframe or minicomputers can now be done on microcomputers. This applies, especially, to computer graphics.

A computer system has five basic elements:

1. An *input system,* such as a keyboard, a joystick, or a scanner
2. An *output system,* such as a printer, a cathode ray tube (familiarly known as a monitor), a plotter, or synthetic speech
3. A *peripheral storage system,* such as a floppy disk, a hard disk, or magnetic tape
4. *Software*—either the disk operating software (DOS) that runs the computer or task software, which enables the computer to do various things, such as word processing or creating graphics
5. The computer itself

It was the development of the microprocessor or "computer on a chip" that made it possible to produce inexpensive personal (or micro) computers. Microcomputers can be distinguished from minicomputers, which can cost from around ten thousand dollars to hundreds of thousands of dollars, and mainframe computers, which can cost from hundreds of thousands of dollars to millions of dollars.

In recent years, the price of computers has fallen dramatically. A personal computer (one that uses Microsoft DOS or Windows 95) with a Pentium chip, an extremely large hard disk, a modem, a color monitor, and a number of software programs can be purchased for around a thousand dollars. Every year, the price of computers goes down and their speed and capabilities go up. And as computers get more powerful, so does the software. One of the most famous archetypes of the powerful computer is HAL, the computer in the movie *2001* (Figure 9.1).

Many computers use software programs—paint programs, animation programs, morphing programs, and multimedia authoring toolkits—to manipulate images in ways that formerly were possible only with enormously

▌FIGURE 9.1
Notice how the astronaut
is in the center of all the
vectors in this scene from
Stanley Kubrick's classic
film, *2001: A Space Odyssey* (1968). A number of
critics have argued, as the
image here suggests, that
the computer HAL is the
real star of the film.

expensive machines. Every week, a new program or a new version of an old program is introduced. And magazines like *PC Graphics & Video* are full of articles about new software, new scanners, and so on.

Windows has, in recent years, more or less usurped the place of the Macintosh computer and marginalized it, even for those doing graphics. Currently, only around 5 percent of computers sold are Macintoshes, despite the fact that its operating system is generally held to be superior to Windows 95 for graphics and image manipulation. Also, powerful workstations manufactured by companies such as Sun Microsystems are used for *computer-aided design* (CAD) and other applications involving images. Personal computers are growing increasingly more powerful, and many personal computers now have as much power as low-end workstations. A kind of convergence takes place.

This means that people who use computers to create and manipulate images have increasingly powerful and inexpensive computers and software programs to work with. For example, the computer I use at home came with *Photoshop, HSC Digital Morph, Aldus Photostyler, Kodak Precision Color Configure,* and *Kai's Power Tools,* among the other software programs—all part of a CD-ROM drive package from Creative Labs. Some of their packages contain video capture cards as well. In sum, there have been incredible changes in recent years, and now a person with an inexpensive system, such as a Pentium 100, has a capacity for image making and image manipulation that he or she could only dream about just a few years ago.

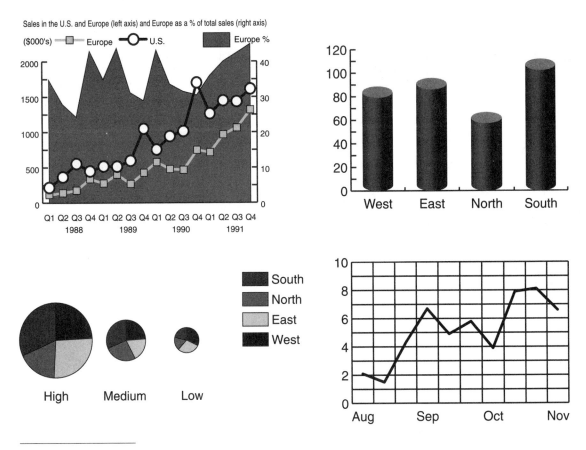

Charts. These charts were generated on a micro-computer. Charts, graphs, and diagrams show relationships visually and thus are able to convey a great deal of information in an economical manner.

COMPUTER GRAPHICS SOFTWARE

There are many different kinds of graphics that computers can generate. It all depends on what the user wants to do. For example, many inexpensive "print shop" software programs enable people to create greeting cards, announcements, posters, and drawings. One can purchase "clip art" to use with these programs—*clip art* being collections of already drawn images that come in their own programs. (You take an image from the hundreds that are available in the clip art program and insert it in your greeting card or announcement with a click of a mouse button or a key on your keyboard.) Frequently, users can manipulate this image and make it larger or smaller, to suit their purposes. Some programs enable people to make large signs or banners. Also, so-called paint programs enable people to do animation and to achieve all kinds of special effects with images.

One of the most common uses of graphics in the business world is for illustrating reports and other material with *charts, tables,* and *graphs.* These charts, tables, and graphs "visualize" data and organize material so that people can make sense of it, very quickly. They show relationships particularly well (Figure 9.2).

INFOGRAPHICS

Infographics is a combination of two words—information and graphics—that suggests how strong the relation is between the two phenomena. Much of what we call "information" (statistics and data) is based on relationships. For example, suppose we are told that 50 percent of Americans earn $15,000 a year. That piece of information doesn't tell us very much. Is $15,000 a lot or a little? What does this figure mean? (We might think of information as involving data put into some kind of relationship, given a context of some nature.)

If we are told that 50 percent of American workers earn $15,000 while 10 percent earn $50,000 and 5 percent earn $100,000 and 35 percent earn $10,000, we now can place that figure in perspective. But if we are given this information in these words, it takes a good deal of mental work to make sense of the numbers. Graphics such as bar charts, pie diagrams, tables, and the like have a unique power to *show* relationships visually. We can see the relationships instantly, instead of having to do mental calculations.

Examine, for example, Figure 9.3, which shows a great deal of information graphically. Because computers have made creation of charts and diagrams so easy, newspapers and television newscasts now use them regularly.

▍ **FIGURE 9.3**
Infographics. These simple diagrams convey a great deal of information. Infographics are now found in many newspapers and publications.

DESKTOP PUBLISHING

Before the development of desktop publishing, organizations that wanted to produce professional-looking printed materials (reports, brochures, newsletters, and so on) had to rely on artists (to draw pictures, make charts and

Brainstorms

Ideas, Opinions, and Speculations from the Mind of Howard Rheingold

Virtual Communities seem to be one of my themes this year. I wrote about them in my report to the U.S. Congress Office of Technology Assessment, and I wrote an essay about them for next Winter's *Whole Earth Review.* An expansion of the WER piece will appear in *Excursions to the Far side of the Mind*, a book of essays that William Morrow will publish in 1988. Here's a Rheingold's Digest version.

Howard Rheingold
• writes
• edits
• consults

His current books:
• *Tools for Thought*
• *Cognitive Connection*
• *Higher Creativity*

...and more on the way

• • •

What is a Virtual Community?

Because I'm a writer, I used to spend my days alone in my room with my words and my thoughts. After work, I would reenter the human community via my neighborhood, my family, my circle of personal and professional acquaintances. But I felt isolated during the working day, and my work provided few opportunities to expand my circle of friends and colleagues. For the past two years, however, I have participated in a wide-ranging, intellectually stimulating, professionally rewarding, and often intensely emotional exchange with dozens of new friends and hundreds of colleagues. And I still spend my days in a room, physically isolated. My mind, however, is linked with a worldwide collection of like-minded (and not so like-minded) souls: My virtual community.

A virtual community is a group of people who may or may not meet one another face to face, and who exchange words and ideas through the mediation of computer bulletin boards and networks. It usually has a geographically local focus and a connection to a much wider domain. The local focus of my virtual community, The Whole Earth 'Lectronic Link (aka "The Well") is the San Francisco Bay Area; the wider locus consists of tens of thousands of other sites around the world, and hundreds of thousands of other people, linked via exchanges of messages into a meta-community known as the Usenet.

The existence of computer-linked communities was predicted twenty years ago by J.C.R. Licklider, who planned the first such community, the ARPAnet: "What will on-line interactive communities be like?" Licklider wrote in 1968: "In most fields they will consist of geographically separated members, sometimes grouped in small clusters and sometimes working individually. They will be communities not of common location, but of common interest..."

My friends and I are part of the future that Licklider dreamed about, and we can attest to the truth of his prediction that "life will be happier for the on-line individual because the people with whom one interacts most strongly will be selected more by commonality of interests and goals than by accidents of proximity."

My community is both a sacred place, in the sense that I visit it for the sheer pleasure of communicating with my friends, and a practical instrument, in the sense that I use it to scan and gather information on subjects that are of momentary or enduring importance, from childcare to neuroscience, technical questions on telecommunications to arguments on philosophical, political, or spiritual subjects. It's a bit like a neighborhood pub or coffee house: Although I don't have to move from my desk, there's a certain sense of place to it. It's a little like a salon, where I can participate in a hundred ongoing

Brainstorms is published by Howard Rheingold • 306 Poplar • Mill Valley, CA • 94941 • (415) 388-3912
©1987 by Howard Rheingold. All rights reserved.

graphs, and do pasteups) and printers (to set typewritten material into type and print it).

Several things led to the growth of *desktop publishing.* First, *laser printers* were developed, which were relatively inexpensive (selling for several thousand dollars) and which offered much better resolution than did conventional *dot matrix printers.* Second, powerful new software programs, such as *Quark Xpress* and *PageMaker,* enabled people to integrate and manipulate textual and visual material with relative ease.

The best desktop publishing software programs have "What You See Is What You Get" (*WYSIWYG,* as it is popularly known) capabilities. This

Figure 9.5
Diagram of a plane. This image was created using *AutoCad,* the leading computer-aided design and drafting (CADD) software program.

means that people using them can see, on the monitor, exactly what the pages they lay out will look like when they are printed out. These programs allow users to adjust the format of the page, the size of the type fonts, the spacing between characters and lines, and so on. The programs also allow users to "import" texts and graphics generated by other programs and print everything on a laser printer or phototypesetter.

The development of desktop publishing means that users can save a great deal of money, because they no longer need to pay artists or printers to create reports, newsletters, brochures, booklets—or even books. Thus, executives can generate material just the way they want it and not have to wait for anyone else to work on (and perhaps modify) their material. Desktop publishing saves money and time and has revolutionized the way individuals and organizations go about creating and publishing material (Figure 9.4).

COMPUTER-AIDED DESIGN AND DRAFTING (CADD)

Computers are also an enormous aid to engineers and architects, and the creation of computer-aided design software programs has had an enormous impact on industry. These programs are replacing drafting and designing by hand; they are, in effect, electronic drafting and designing programs that enable architects, engineers, and others to create and manipulate images in remarkable ways. By using various CADD programs, it is possible to generate wire-frame (line) drawings of buildings and devices and then shade them in or render them in color to see what they actually will look like (Figure 9.5).

And once a drawing is made and memorized, it can be rotated so that designers can see what it will look like from different angles.

Most programs are pixel-oriented, but some newer ones are object-
oriented. They use pixels to create lines and shapes, but the computer "mem-
orizes" these figures; and when they are enlarged or manipulated, the programs produce sharper images than pixel-oriented ones do. Computers and
new software programs also make it easier to do animation, as the rabbits in
Figure 9.6 demonstrate.

COMPUTER VIDEOGAMES

The ability of the computer to generate images (and sound) has been an
important factor in the development of videogames. The first games, such as
Pong, which appeared in 1972, were very elemental ones that had little in the
way of animation or special effects. In *Pong,* one played table tennis with an
electronic blip. As the technology developed and computers became both
less expensive and more powerful, computer videogames have become much
more elaborate and interesting.

The images are now more realistic; the colors are richer and subtler; there
is less distortion; and the games themselves are more complicated and chal-
lenging. The quality of the images in these games is affected by the power of
the computer it is played on and the capabilities of the monitor being used.
The same computer game projects different images on different computers
and monitors. But even without the most optimal systems, games such as
PacMan and *Flight Simulator* were able to captivate millions of Americans and
stimulate the development of ever more sophisticated games and systems.

SPECIAL EFFECTS

Many of us do not realize the impact that computers have had on the media.
When we watch a television program, many of the things we see (in the
beginning, for example, where titles move and flip around) are special video
effects; commercials also use them extensively. In addition, video has invaded

■ FIGURE 9.7

Luxo, Jr. These images were created using extremely powerful computers and software imaging programs. The Luxo images are from an animated film.

film, and many of the effects we see in movies were generated by video. For example, the science fiction film *Tron* had about twenty minutes of video effects in it. And, of course, Music Television (MTV) is full of these video effects.

These effects are created by very powerful computing systems and programs (Figure 9.7). But even the ordinary personal computer, outfitted with a graphics card and using an inexpensive software program, can generate many interesting effects, including the following (Figure 9.8):

1. *Mirroring.* The computer takes an image and creates a mirror image of it. With some machines, multiple mirror images can be created on one screen, and the mirrors can be overlapped if desired.
2. *Mosaic.* The computer takes an image and maps squares onto the image, simulating a mosaic.
3. *Strobe.* A freeze effect of an image is held for a short time and released as another is frozen. This stylized effect dramatizes movement within the screen.
4. *Cut and paste.* Video artists can capture sections of an image and place them elsewhere on the image, while manipulating color, shape, and size. In some cases, cutouts can be combined with a live image.
5. *Painting.* A still image is overlaid with color in many different ways, using many different brush techniques to create this effect.
6. *Shattered image.* An image is fractured into slivers or other shapes and shown in this state.
7. *Posterization.* This process involves increasing image contrast (luminance value), which produces, at the extreme, a cartoonlike quality.
8. *Stenciling.* A shape, regular or irregular, can be created to protect areas of the screen from a given effect; or it can be used in the reverse to dictate where the effect goes.
9. *Chroma-key.* This process electronically removes red, blue, or green from an image and replaces it with a different color or image.

(a)

(b)

(c)

(d)

▌ FIGURE 9.8
Bob Malecki, "Special Effects." These special effects were all created by sophisticated computer imaging processes. These images are (a) an unmodified photo of Jan, (b) a mosaic, also known as a pixelated image, (c) a solarized or painted image, and (d) a frame move repeated with varying degrees of image wash.

10. *Digitization.* This process puts an image into computer memory for subsequent manipulation.
11. *Animation.* Computers and new software programs also make it easier to do animation (see Figure 9.6).

These are some of the most common effects that can be created by computers. In addition to being used for artistic purposes, computers also are playing an increasingly important role in medicine, where various kinds of imaging processes have been developed. These processes allow physicians to gain valuable information about patients without having to use "intrusive" means (such as exploratory surgery). As a result of these new imaging processes, when it is necessary to operate, surgeons have much more precise information on hand before they begin.

E-MAIL AND THE INTERNET

E-mail (electronic mail) is one of the most important new developments connected with computers. In recent years, we've come to recognize that the computer is not just an amazingly fast instrument for calculating figures or a powerful device for writing and formatting text and for creating and manipulating images; it is also a communication device. In fact, that may well be its most important function.

E-mail now competes with regular mail—also known as "snail mail"—and is replacing regular mail in a number of cases. With *e-mail,* one can "correspond" electronically with people all over the world and have one's message relayed in an instant.

For example, it used to take some three or four weeks to get a reply to a letter sent abroad—and sometimes even longer than that. But with e-mail, you can get a reply the same day, in many cases. It is also possible to send the same message to a number of people, so communication among people with certain common interest areas is now greatly facilitated. Of course, there is the problem of getting too many e-mail messages, or what might be called "junk e-mail." It is not unusual for some people to find fifty or more e-mail messages when they turn on their computers. The only thing you don't get with e-mail are the beautiful stamps found in some countries, but many post offices now use electronic stamping devices, so even that pleasure is waning.

E-mail is possible because the *Internet* now links people all over the world in an electronic network. The development of certain software programs, such as *Mosaic* and later *Netscape,* has made the Internet the most revolutionary and exciting communications medium in recent years. Many institutions and organizations now have Web sites on the World Wide Web (the term is most significant) where people "surfing" the Internet can get information about everything from stock market prices to course offerings at universities. You can now electronically browse through bookstores and order books and numerous other products and services on the Internet—as well as make phone calls, connect with political parties and presidential candidates, and so on. Many individuals have their own pages on the Internet, too. It seems that Marshall McLuhan's prediction that communication technologies were creating a "global village" has come true.

As a sign of the Internet's importance, the Microsoft Corporation, in a massive corporate turnabout, decided to focus its attention on the Internet and now is waging a major battle for dominance with Netscape.

It is important to remember that the Internet is not just a print medium. People can use images, sound, color, and even videos for their Web pages on the Internet. Thus, there is an aesthetic dimension to be considered when creating Web sites. In art schools, for instance, for many artists, the computer is now much more important than the tube of oil paint. (There is also the problem of having to wait while images download, which exasperates many people who use the Internet.) In any case, the Internet has opened up a whole new world of opportunities for the exchange of information and ideas.

COMPUTER ANIMATION

Computer animation gained prominence in 1982 when Disney's *Tron* was released—a technological triumph but a box office disappointment. The film recounts the adventures of a videogame ace who gets sucked into a computer and must battle various villains to escape from it. It had approximately twenty minutes of computer animation in it, along with, curiously, hand-painted frames. (Some 75,000 frames were individually handled, and 500 people were involved in postproduction aspects of the film.) Unfortunately, despite its remarkable computer graphics, it was a somewhat dull and uninteresting film—perhaps too much like a video game for viewers.

To date, approximately fifty films have used computer animation to varying degrees, including *2001, The Last Starfighter, The Abyss,* and *Young Sherlock Holmes.* But it was *Terminator II: Judgment Day* that captured the public's attention and that represents a truly successful use of computer animation. Perhaps the most celebrated aspect of the film involves the T-1000, the liquid metal cyborg that "melts" into a corridor floor and that re-forms its human image after being blown apart by shotgun blasts. Of course, it cost $100 million to make the film, so using computers is not necessarily a money-saving technology. For example, in *Terminator II,* it took approximately thirty-five computer animators almost a year to produce the images of T-1000—images that appeared on the screen for about five minutes.

Disney's *Toy Story,* a huge box office success, is the first fully computer animated film and is likely to lead to a new era in animated films. Pixar, the company that produced the animation, used twenty-seven animators to create the seventy-six characters in the seventy-five-minute film.

Computer animators work with what might be called "digital clay" by drawing an image on a computer screen in a wire-mesh shape that can be easily manipulated. Once the shape is given its final form for a given frame, it is colored. The computer can then generate realistic highlights, shadows, and reflections for that image.

In some cases, the artists convert a film image to digital form that is displayed on a computer screen. This means that artists, using various graphics programs, can modify the image, pixel by pixel, to suit their needs. The biggest problem computer animators face is making their images believable.

If audiences don't see the images as realistic, they tend to lose interest very quickly. And computer animators still have trouble reproducing realistic-looking facial expressions and skin tones.

The process known as *morphing* is becoming more and more popular. (*Morphology* means "the study of structure," and the word *morphe* is Greek for "to shape or to form.") Morphing involves transforming images from their original state into a different one in successive stages. (Cartoonists have used morphing for years, transforming a character's face in successive frames.) For example, a man's face can be transformed into an animal's (or vice versa). In a well-known horror film, *The Wolf Man,* made in 1942, a series of superimposed film shots showed Lon Chaney's face being transformed into that of a wolflike monster. Now, inexpensive computer programs make morphing extremely easy, and morphing is found in more and more films, television programs, and commercials. There is also a process known as *warphing* (a combination of *warping* and *morphing*), which involves bending and twisting images as they are being morphed.

Using computer animation, filmmakers can create whatever images they want. Anything is possible now—we can have films with famous actresses and actors who are only invented images, and we can have films in which dead actors and actresses interact with live ones (as occurs in some commercials now). But that doesn't mean that the films these filmmakers create using computer animation are necessarily worth watching. In the final analysis, films—like other works of art in other media—require good stories, with interesting characters and exciting plots. It is the writing that is crucial, and all the special effects in the world can't save an inferior story.

There also may be something in computer technology that deadens works, that drains the vitality out of them; these animated segments may fascinate filmmakers so much that they lose sight of the other elements needed to make a successful film. What computer animation does is to enlarge the possibilities open to those who make films. But when it comes to films, television programs, and other narrative works, the most important computer software is not the animation software, but the word-processing/script-writing software. It isn't technology that creates great films, but imagination and creativity on the part of writers and brilliance on the part of performers.

CONCLUSIONS

Have all of the remarkable video effects that computers can generate led to an important new kind of art, or are computer effects essentially one more form of "commercial art," and not really a serious art medium? This is a subject of much debate.

▌ FIGURE 9.9

Detail from *Pixellage*, 1983. Choreography by Betty Erickson. Music by A. Corelli. This ballet, appropriately named, used computer-generated images to create remarkable effects.

Video is still a relatively new medium, so we must give it time to develop and not make any premature judgments. At the same time, a great deal of work has been done in video, so its potentialities should be discernible (Figure 9.9).

Michael Noll, who was one of the first people to write about the subject, expressed a great deal of optimism about the medium in an essay "Computers and the Visual Arts," written in 1967: "In the computer, man has created not just an inanimate tool but an intellectual and active creative partner that, when fully exploited, could be used to produce wholly new art forms and possibly new aesthetic experiences." By 1982, however, Noll had serious reservations. As he wrote in the art show catalogue of a SIGGRAPH (Special Interest Group on Computer Graphics):

> It is in its use as a serious artistic medium in the visual arts where the digital computer has not yet achieved its anticipated potential. Digital computers are being used to create visual imagery, but many people feel that something is missing.

The images sometimes appear to be attempts to mimic other media. Many are cold and sterile and are somewhat devoid of human expression. Randomness combines with geometric structure to create designs that are frequently interesting but that are little more. One is frequently left with the impression that many patterns are simply experiments in learning the new medium.

Noll raises the question as to whether there is some kind of fundamental antithesis between technology and the arts, between machines and what might be called "the human spirit" (Figure 9.10).

What will happen with video remains to be seen. There are serious video artists who are experimenting with video and trying to create works of sig-

■ FIGURE 9.10

(a) Michael Noll, *Computer Composition with Lines,* 1964.
(b) Piet Mondrian, *Composition with Lines,* 1917. The computer-generated image (A) was created to be very similar to (b), Mondrian's work. When Noll showed audiences the two images, labeling them "A" and "B," and asked which was the Mondrian, large percentages thought that the computer-generated image (A) was the Mondrian. This occurred because, it is hypothesized, the computer-generated image was more irregular or random than the Mondrian painting. Another of Mondrian's paintings, *Composition with Blue and Yellow,* is shown in Figure 0.6.

(a)

(b)
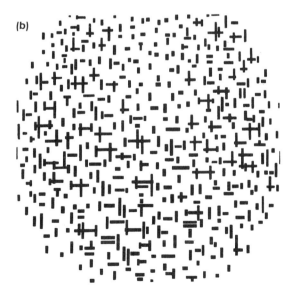

nificance. But how different is their work from film or television, except for the greater use of special effects?

The future will tell us what to make of computer art and video. For the moment, computers enable people to create and manipulate images of all sorts in remarkable ways. Whether this technology will develop into a "serious" art that creates ennobling works of lasting quality remains to be seen.

APPLICATIONS

1. What impact do you think computers have had on society? (If you have a computer, what effect has it had on your life?) Be as specific as you can in answering this question.

2. In what ways have computers directly impacted on your life? Make a list of particulars and briefly explain each item. You might take one day in your life and see where and how computers are involved with your activities, either directly or indirectly.

3. Newspapers often run stories about young students, known as "hackers," who use their computers to get into the computer systems of the military or other large organizations. What do you think motivates these hackers? What should be done to hackers who are caught?

4. If you have access to a computer, use it to create a newsletter to give to your friends. Decide on a title, a topic, and a format. (If you don't have a desktop publishing program, you can make a pasteup with printed matter from the computer and artwork you do by hand.) Did the computer facilitate the process?

5. If you have access to a computer, play some games on it for an hour. Write a short essay describing what the experience was like. What were the graphics like? What about the plot? Did you enjoy it? Why or why not?

6. Play sociologist. Go to a videogame arcade and survey the players. What questions should you ask them? Make sure some of the questions involve obtaining quantitative data. When you are done, examine the data and write a report describing what you found and explaining what it means.

7. Watch *Tron,* which contains about twenty minutes of computer animation. Write a review of the film, focusing on its aesthetic aspects. What, if anything, worked in the film? What were its drawbacks? How would you have improved it?

GLOSSARY

A-B axis The axis that goes from the left side of a screen to the right side. (See *Z-axis*.)

Aesthetics The branch of philosophy concerned with questions related to the nature of the beautiful: what is the relationship between truth and beauty, between form and content, and so on. Applied aesthetics, in contrast, is interested in how to obtain certain effects through the use of color, lighting, certain camera shots, editing, and so on.

Analogy A mode of communication in which meaning is generated by making comparisons. Metaphors are based on analogies, as are similes, which are weaker forms of analogies.

Animation The process of filming drawings or clay sculptures to generate the illusion of motion; literally means "giving life to."

Association A mode of communication, such as metonymy and synecdoche (a weaker form of metonymy), in which meaning is generated by using associations, connections people have in their minds between two things.

Asymmetrical See *informal balance*.

Autoeroticism In aesthetics, sensual pleasure caused by contemplation of one's image.

Axial balance Formal balance in which elements in a visual field are arranged symmetrically on both sides of an axis.

Balance The arrangement of elements in a visual field that produces a sense of order and stability.

Bicameral brain The two hemispheres of the brain, each of which has certain characteristics. The left hemisphere is associated with logic and is linear; the right hemisphere is associated with imagination and is holistic.

CAD (computer-aided design) Software programs that enable users such as architects and engineers to create designs on computers and manipulate the images for various purposes. There are now CADD (computer-aided design and drafting) programs as well, for draftspersons and others.

Caricature A form of humorous drawing that captures the likeness of a person but exaggerates and distorts various features of that person.

Cartoon A drawing, usually in one frame, depicting some kind of humorous situation, which is generally accompanied by a caption.

Chart A means of presenting information in visual form so that relationships can immediately be seen.

Chiaroscuro lighting A form of lighting characterized by very strong lights and darks, as opposed to flat lighting, which diminishes the differences be-tween lights and darks.

Chroma-key The process of electronically removing red, blue, or green from a computer image and re-placing it with a different color or image.

Clip art Software programs that contain drawings and other visual phenomena that can be used in preparing newsletters, reports, and any other kind of desktop publishing.

Close-up A film or television camera shot that shows a person's head. There are also extreme close-ups, which show only part of a person's face. Many people suggest that because of its small screen size, television is a close-up medium.

Codes Ways of interpreting signs and symbols and organizing behavior. There are highway codes, which are known and which people are tested on, and aesthetic codes, which often escape our aware-ness but also often shape our behavior.

Color The description we use for things based on the way light is reflected or emitted from objects. Colors are differentiated in terms of hue, satura-tion, and brightness. We also distinguish between primary colors—red, yellow, and blue—and sec-ondary colors—orange, green, and purple.

Colorization The capacity of certain computers and software programs to modify the colors in images. As a result of this process, black-and-white films and television programs can be turned into color, though there is a great deal of dispute about the propriety of doing so.

Comic strip A popular art form, generally found in newspapers, characterized by continuing charac-ters, a number of panels, and dialogue presented in balloons. Comic strips can be either serious or hu-morous and often are extremely long-lived.

Composition The arrangement of elements in a visual field so as to please the eye or obtain an intended effect.

Condensation The psychological process by which the mind unifies and pulls together disparate im-ages in dreams so as to avoid the dream censor. The condensed image generally has a sexual dimension to it, though this is not apparent. We also react to the sexual content of condensed images when we are awake, though we do not create these images.

Contrast A difference between two visual elements (such as simple and complicated, dull and bright, or dark and light) to generate emphasis.

Cool medium One that provides relatively few data and thus generates strong involvement on the part of the viewer or listener.

Cut and paste Process whereby video artists capture sections of an image and place them elsewhere in the image while manipulating color, shape, and size.

Depth of field The capacity of a camera to keep ob-jects, located at different distances from it, in fo-cus. Depth of field can vary, based on the f-stop of the camera, the focal length of the lens, and the distance from the camera to the object being photographed.

Desktop publishing The use of computers, power-ful software programs that enable users to manip-ulate textual and visual material, and laser printers to produce high-quality printed matter (such as re-ports, pamphlets, books, and so on).

Digitized image An image put into a computer that can then be manipulated for various purposes.

Direction The line of movement of some aspect of an image. These directions are sometimes known as vectors.

Displacement The psychological process by which the mind invests an object or symbol with signifi-cance taken from some other object or symbol. Fre-quently, this significance has a sexual dimension to it, and the displaced objects often are similar (in shape or function) to the object that is displaced.

Dot A small, round mark. Dots are made by the in-tersection of two lines. Computers generate dots (on monitors) that are called pixels.

Dot-matrix printer A kind of printer, used with computers, that uses dots to form letters and other visual material. The typical dot-matrix printer gen-erates 75 dots per inch, in contrast to the laser printer, which produces 300 dots per inch.

Drama A narrative or story, usually involving strong emotions and conflict among or between characters and the resolution of the conflict by action.

Editing The process in film or television that takes place after images have been taken by a camera. Editing involves putting together the various elements or components of a film or television program in a manner that produces the impact and effect desired. This often involves cutting (eliminating) some material and splicing bits and pieces together. Editing is often done manually in films, but new devices have been developed that enable the editing process to be done electronically.

E-mail   Messages sent by people with computers and modems via the Internet.

Evidence   The notion that visual images can be relied on to tell the truth about something or some event. Now that computers can manipulate images and photographs so easily, visual images no longer are seen as reliable—seeing can no longer be equated with truthfulness and accuracy.

Figure-ground   A relationship between an object and the background against which we see the object. The background affects the meaning figures have, because they often are ambiguous.

Film frame   The basic unit of a film. The frame, in essence, is a photographic negative of a static image. Film is projected at twenty-four frames per second, which—because of a visual phenomenon known as an afterimage—produces the illusion of movement.

Flat lighting   Lighting in which differences between lights and darks are minimized or flattened. The opposite of *chiaroscuro* lighting.

Flush left   Type lined up in a straight line on the left margin of a page. Flush right involves lining it up in a straight line on the right margin of a page. Textual matter in books and magazines is generally flush left and flush right or "justified." Ragged right, in which lines do not line up in a straight line, is held by many typographers to give a more modern or contemporary look to a page.

Focus   The clarity or sharpness of an image. Soft focus generates images that are not precise and clear and produces a dreamlike effect.

Formal balance   See *axial balance*.

Freeze-frame   The capacity of computers using certain software programs to capture an image and keep it immobile, or maintained as if it has been frozen. Freeze-frame is also used in film to suggest arrested motion and to generate a feeling of surprise or shock.

Genre   Kinds of stories, programs, or films. We make a distinction between a medium (film, television, and so on) and the kind of programs or genres in a given medium. For example, the medium of television includes many genres: soap operas, quiz shows, sports shows, interview shows, news shows, documentaries, and so on.

Gestalt   The psychological process by which we combine a number of disparate elements into a whole that is greater than the sum of its parts and whose properties cannot be derived from the various parts. We commonly use the term to mean "putting things together" and getting some kind of an insight.

Glamorization   The process by which we invest people or objects with qualities that we find appealing and desirable. A photographer can glamorize through the use of lighting, background, camera angles, and filtering devices.

Grain   The prominence of the minute dots that make up a photograph: the more dots used in a photograph, the less grainy it is.

Graph   A form of visual display showing quantitative relationships, often in the form of bars or points on a field.

Grid layout   A collection of crisscrossing lines that make simple forms. These grid forms are used to help people without much knowledge of design format visual material in an attractive manner and avoid mistakes. Some desktop publishing software programs come with grids in them and include advice about good layout.

Haptical   The term used by art historian Alois Riegl for finding pleasure in the texture and grain of objects.

Hot medium   One that provides a lot of data and thus fails to generate strong involvement on the part of the viewer or listener.

Icon   In semiotic analysis, something that communicates meaning by resemblance. Thus, a photograph is iconic because it resembles the person who's been photographed.

Illustration   The use of drawings, paintings, or other visual material to exemplify, give focus to, or decorate textual material.

Image   A visual representation of something or someone. Images can be thought of as being complex pictorial phenomena, often having symbolic significance and unconscious meanings. Image also refers to the concept we have about someone or something.

Imagination   The ability of the mind to create new ideas and images or to visualize things not present. The term suggests that there is a link between images or visual phenomena and creative behavior.

Index   Signs that signify by logic or causal connection, as in the case of smoke and fire.

Informal balance   Elements of a composition that are not arranged equally on both sides of imaginary axes.

Information overload   A numbness and inability to process information caused by overexposure to it.

Internet   The open interconnection of networks through which connected computers can transmit visual and sound data. The most popular uses of the Internet are for transmitting electronic mail and for finding information on the World Wide Web.

Intertextuality   Commonly understood to refer to the fact that works in the arts (or "texts," in the language of semiotics) often borrow from or are related in various ways to other texts. For example, a parody imitates and makes fun of another work.

Jump cut   A quick cut from one scene to another that leaves out some intermediate scenes and thus speeds the action.

Laser printer   A printer, commonly used in desktop publishing, that offers relatively high resolution—300 or more dots per square inch.

Layout   See *composition.*

Logo   A design, sometimes made of letters, used by an organization as a means of establishing its identity.

Metaphor   A figure of speech indicating an analogy or similarity between two things—for example, "My love is a rose." (See *simile.*)

Metonymy   A method of generating meaning through the use of association. For example, a mansion suggests wealth (and good taste).

Mirroring   In computer graphics, a method of creating mirror images of an image.

Montage   A series of images and sounds that, when combined in a certain way, generate a powerful effect.

Morphing   The process of restructuring images, in minute stages, so they turn into images of something, or in the case of individuals, someone else.

Mosaic   A form of pictorial representation in which an image is created out of small, colored pieces of stone or some other material. This effect can also be created by computers with the right imaging software.

Movement   A sense of activity or change in position. It is created in films and television by the actions of characters and in static visual fields by use of line, shape, lighting, and color.

Music television (MTV)   Videos, generally performed by music groups, that either dramatize a song or show it being performed. Many of these videos use avant-garde film techniques.

Narcotization   A sense of deadness and boredom created, for example, by watching too much television, which can prevent the alternating of left-brain and right-brain activity.

Optical   The term used by art historian Alois Riegl for scanning objects according to their outline.

Optical illusion   A visual image that confuses the viewer and is deceptive.

Painting   In computer graphics, a still image overlaid with color in many different ways.

Persistence of vision   The process that enables us to connect the frames of a film and "see" the film as continuous.

Perspective   The ability to represent objects that are three-dimensional and give a sense of depth on a two-dimensional plane.

Phallic symbol   Any object that, for one reason or another, such as resemblance in shape or similarity in function, suggests the male sex organ.

Pica   A unit of measurement in type equivalent to 12 points or approximately one-sixth of an inch.

Pixel   An abbreviation of "picture element." Essentially, a point or dot that is shown on a computer monitor and that is the building block out of which lines, shapes, and images are created.

Plotter   A printing device used to reproduce drawings, architectural renderings, and other visual phenomena using computers and graphics software programs.

Point A unit of measurement in typography equal to approximately 1/72 inch. Twelve points make a pica.

Pose A particular posture for a portrait or photograph that reflects feelings and attitudes and generates a desired image.

Posterization Process by which video artists increase image contrast.

Postmodern A term for works that use a number of different styles and that abandon a traditional linear narrative.

Proportion A relationship between elements in a visual field in which a part is considered with respect to the whole.

Psyche The mind in all its conscious and unconscious functions and capacities, as a center of thoughts, emotions, and behavior. Freud suggested that the psyche is made up of an id (drives), a superego (conscience), and an ego (rationality) that mediates between the two opposing forces—the id and superego.

Psychological closure The way the mind combines elements into wholes and completes visual phenomena that are incomplete.

Reaction shot A television or film shot showing a person's reactions (by facial expression) to some event. These shots generate a sense of drama and excitement.

Reverse print White type on a black background (or some variation on that theme), instead of the usual black type on a white background.

Roman typeface A typeface characterized by upright letters, lines of varying thicknesses, and serifs.

Saccades The quick, intermittent movements the eye makes when it fixes on one point after another in a visual field. Each saccade lasts approximately one-twentieth of a second.

Sans serif typeface A typeface without serifs, the little marks that finish off the main strokes of letters in certain typefaces.

Scale A relationship of size between objects or elements in a visual field.

Scanner A device that can input graphics or textual material directly into a computer.

Selective perception The process by which people tend to see only certain things in a given situation. They focus on material of interest to them and neglect other things that are present.

Semiotics The science of signs that investigates the way meaning is produced and transmitted. (See *sign*.)

Serif typeface A typeface that uses short cross-lines at the ends of letters.

Shape The visible configuration or outward form of something.

Shattered image An image broken into pieces to achieve a desired aesthetic effect through the use of computers and imaging software.

Shot angle The angle at which a photo, film, or television shot is taken; used to promote an effect or feeling in viewers.

Sign One of the basic concepts of semiotics. A sign is anything that can be used to stand for something else. Words, images, facial expressions, clothing, hairstyles—just about everything can be seen as a sign. The way signs work and the problems connected with signs are the subject matter of semiotics.

Signifier/signified According to Ferdinand de Saussure, the division of signs into signifiers (sounds or objects) and signifieds (the concepts generated by the signifier). The relationship between signifiers and signifieds is arbitrary or conventional.

Simile A figure of speech, using "like" or "as," in which a weak relationship between two subjects is posited—for example, "My love is like a rose." (See *metaphor*.)

Sound effects The use of made-up sounds or noises (generally in dramatic presentations) to simulate real sounds and noises and generate emotional responses and a sense of verisimilitude in those who hear them.

Spatiality The sense of space, determined in large part by the amount of "white" space, in a visual field.

Stenciling In computer graphics, the process by which shapes are created to protect areas of the screen from a given effect or to dictate where the effect should go.

Strobe A special effect characterized by short, bright pulses of light turning on and off.

Supergraphics   Use of letters and words and other visual phenomena on a very large scale.

Surrealism   A twentieth-century artistic (and literary) movement that attempted to capture the working of the subconscious by using fantastic imagery and trying to approximate a dreamlike state.

Symbol   A form of sign, for Peirce, in which the meaning is conventional and must be learned. In ordinary use, anything that stands for something else, often on the basis of convention or association.

Symmetrical   See *formal balance.*

Synecdoche   A form of metonymy in which the part stands for the whole or the whole for the part. Thus, the Pentagon is used to stand for the American military establishment and the White House for the presidency in the United States.

Table   A visual means of presenting numerical relationships among data, generally in columns and rows.

Talking heads   Television programs in which there is little physical action and basically nothing but conversation takes place.

Typography   The art of selecting and using typefaces for maximum effect. It also involves such matters as the composition of the page and the sizing of illustrations and other graphics.

Unity   A sense of harmoniousness and wholeness created by the relationships of elements in a visual field.

WYSIWYG (What You See Is What You Get)   The ability of certain software programs to provide users with an accurate picture of what a page will look like when it is printed out. This feature is of particular importance in desktop publishing.

Zapping   The process of using a remote-control tuner to "flip" from one television station to another. People zapping do not watch programs, but instead, create their own programs from bits and pieces of what is on the air.

Z-axis shot   A shot in which the action is vertical to the screen image and moves toward or away from viewers. This kind of shot is particularly important in television because the screen is so small. (See *A-B axis.*)

Zoom shot   A shot in which the lens of a camera is used to move in on a scene for a closer view (or, in the reverse, move away from a scene). If used too frequently, zoom shots lose their impact and disturb viewers.

SELECTED ANNOTATED BIBLIOGRAPHY

The literature on visual communication is vast. There are an incredible number of books on aesthetics, art, design, graphics, film, television, and related concerns. And with good reason, for if we are "thinking creatures" (homo sapiens), we are also "seeing creatures" (homo oculans). What follows is a listing and brief description of some of the more important and interesting books in the field. A more complete listing of resources (including those cited in the text) follows in the References.

BERGER, ARTHUR ASA. *Li'l Abner: A Study in American Satire.* 1970. Twayne Publishers.
This study deals with the social, cultural, and political significance of one of America's most important comic strips, Li'l Abner. It considers such topics as comics and popular culture, satire, and graphic techniques in the comics.

BERGER, ARTHUR ASA. *The Comic-Stripped American: What Dick Tracy, Blondie, Daddy Warbucks and Charlie Brown Tell Us About Ourselves.* 1973. Walker.
This book analyzes the cultural and symbolic significance of many of America's classic comic strips.

BERGER, ARTHUR ASA. *Signs in Contemporary Culture: An Introduction to Semiotics.* 1984. Longman.
This book explains some of the basic concepts of semi-otic theory and applies them to various topics, many of which involve visual matters.

BERGER, JOHN. *Ways of Seeing.* 1972. Penguin Books.
This book is based on a series of four television broadcasts that the English critic John Berger made for the BBC. It has four written essays (on images, the portrayal of women in art, politics and art, and advertising) and three pictorial ones.

BERGER, JOHN. *About Looking.* 1980. Pantheon Books.
This collection of essays previously appeared in an English magazine, New Society. *The essays deal with such topics as why we look at animals, how we use photography, and what significance various artists and works of art have.*

CLARK, KENNETH. *Looking at Pictures.* 1968. Beacon Press.
This book contains a number of analyses by Clark that are meant to teach us how to look at paintings in as profound and discerning a manner as possible. Clark argues that knowing about a painter's life, his personality and beliefs and values, where the painting fits into a painter's total work, and what the art of his time was like, are necessary to interpret a given work and look at pictures (in general) correctly.

DEKEN, JOSEPH. *Computer Images: State of the Art.* 1983. Stewart, Tabori & Chang.
This book is full of remarkable four-color images generated by computers. It deals with computers and images, the way the computer is affecting our aesthetic sensibilities, the role of computer images and fantasy, and related topics.

DICHTER, ERNEST. *Packaging: The Sixth Sense? A Guide to Identifying Consumer Motivation.* 1975. Cahners Publishing.
Dichter, the father of motivation research, deals with the power of packaging and shows how it is involved with deep-seated psychological anxieties we all experience. The book contains much interesting material on how people interpret symbols and relate to visual phenomena, especially as these matters apply to packaging and "commercial communication."

DONDIS, DONIS A. *A Primer of Visual Literacy.* 1973. M.I.T. Press.
This early textbook on visual communication deals with visual literacy, composition, visual techniques, the way visual arts function, and similar topics. It contains numerous line drawings and other illustrations and offers a good introduction to the principles of design.

EISENSTEIN, SERGEI. *Film Form: Essays in Film Theory.* Edited and translated by Jay Leyda. 1949. Harcourt Brace Jovanovich.
This series of essays by a famous film director focuses on various aspects of film theory. Eisenstein deals with such topics as the nature of film form, film language, montage, and the structure of film. A companion book of essays, Film Sense, *is available from the same publisher.*

FOUCAULT, MICHEL. *This Is Not a Pipe.* 1983. University of California Press.
This fascinating little book deals with the work of the Belgian surrealist, René Magritte. One of his most famous paintings shows a pipe, and underneath it is written "this is not a pipe." Foucault attempts to explain what Magritte's visual non sequiturs mean.

GOWANS, ALAN. *The Unchanging Arts: New Forms for the Traditional Functions of Art in Society.* 1971. J. B. Lippincott.
Gowans deals with the functions of art in society and covers everything from the arts of antiquity to advertising and comic strips. His scope is incredible and his insights are astounding.

GOWANS, ALAN. *Learning to See: Historical Perspective on Modern Popular/Commercial Arts.* 1981. Bowling Green University Popular Press.
This book carries forward and updates the arguments of The Unchanging Arts. *Gowans deals with everything from Chinese junks to soap operas and football. Provocative and fascinating.*

GROTJAHN, MARTIN. *The Voice of the Symbol.* 1971. Delta Books.
This book provides a Freudian psychoanalytic interpretation of many of our most important symbols and addresses such topics as television, dreams, and the work of Hieronymus Bosch.

JUNG, CARL G. (ED.). *Man and His Symbols.* 1964. Dell Books.
This book contains articles by Jung and his followers on the relationship between the symbol and the psyche, with much material on art and other forms of visual communication. Jung elaborated a different psychology from Freud, and it is instructive to see how Jungians analyze things. Profusely illustrated.

KRIS, ERNST. *Psychoanalytic Explorations in Art.* 1964. Schocken Books.
This collection of essays by Kris (sometimes collaborating with other authors) applies psychoanalytic theory to expressive behavior. It has chapters on art and psychoanalysis, the art of the insane, caricature, and the creative process.

KURTZ, BRUCE. *Spots: The Popular Art of American Television Commercials.* 1977. Arts Communications.
This book was written to provide readers with a conceptual framework to understand television commercials. The book shows how commercials work, how they relate to (and borrow from) other works and media. It also includes interviews with some important makers of commercials and analyses of their work.

SONTAG, SUSAN. *On Photography.* 1973. Delta Books.
This series of philosophical essays focuses on the nature of photography, its relation to other art forms, and its social and political significance. It also discusses the work of many important photographers. The book orig-

inally was written as a series of essays in The New York Review of Books. *Provocative and illuminating.*

UDE-PESTEL, ANNELIESE. *Betty: History and Art of a Child in Therapy.* 1977. Science and Behavior Books.
This fascinating book deals with a terribly disturbed child and her paintings and drawings. The book contains twenty-six paintings by Betty that show how she changes as the result of her therapy, from a deeply disturbed child to a "normal" one.

WORTH, SOL. *Studying Visual Communication.* Edited, with an introduction, by Larry Gross. 1981. University of Pennsylvania Press.

This is a collection of scholarly essays by a filmmaker and theorist of visual communication. The essays deal with topics such as the semiotics of film, the nature and functions of symbolism, and the uses of film in education.

ZETTL, HERBERT. *Sight, Sound, Motion: Applied Media Aesthetics.* 1973. Wadsworth Publishing.
This pioneering work, encyclopedic in nature, discusses the principles of aesthetics, with particular reference to film and television. Zettl shows how important a role aesthetic matters—light, color, sound, camera work, and so on—play in the media. Lavishly illustrated.

REFERENCES

Adatto, Kiku. 1993. *Picture Perfect: The Art and Artifice of Public Image Making.* New York: Basic Books.

Albers, Joseph. 1971. *Interaction of Color.* New Haven, Conn.: Yale University Press.

Arnheim, Rudolf. 1953. *Film as Art.* Berkeley: University of California Press.

Arnheim, Rudolf. 1966. *Toward a Psychology of Art.* Berkeley: University of California Press.

Arnheim, Rudolf. 1969. *Visual Thinking.* London: Faber & Faber.

Ashton, Dore. 1989. "The Elemental Fascination of Portrait Photography." *The Chronicle of Higher Education* (April 12).

Aufderheide, Pat. 1987. "The Look of the Sound." In *Watching Television,* ed. Todd Gitlin. New York: Pantheon Books.

Barnhurst, Kevin G. 1994. *Seeing the Newspaper.* New York: St. Martin's Press.

Barthes, Roland. 1957. *Mythologies.* New York: Hill & Wang.

Bassett, Richard. 1969. *The Open Eye in Learning.* Cambridge, Mass.: M.I.T. Press.

Becker, Howard S. 1982. *Art Worlds.* Berkeley: University of California Press.

Behrens, Roy R. 1984. *Design in the Visual Arts.* Englewood Cliffs, N.J.: Prentice-Hall.

Berger, Arthur Asa. 1976. *The Comic-Stripped American.* New York: Walker.

Berger, Arthur Asa. 1982. *Media Analysis Techniques.* Beverly Hills, Calif.: Sage.

Berger, Arthur Asa. 1984. *Signs in Contemporary Culture.* New York: Longman.

Berger, John. 1972. *Ways of Seeing.* New York: Penguin.

Berger, John. 1988. *About Looking.* New York: Pantheon.

Boggs, Joseph M. 1978. *The Art of Watching Films.* Menlo Park, Calif.: Benjamin/Cummings.

Bronowski, J. 1978. *The Visionary Eye.* Cambridge, Mass.: M.I.T. Press.

Bullen, J. B. 1981. *Vision & Design.* London: Oxford University Press.

Carroll, Lewis. 1960. *Alice's Adventures in Wonderland and Through the Looking Glass.* New York: Signet Classics.

Clark, Kenneth. 1960. *Looking at Pictures.* Boston: Beacon Press.

Collier, John. 1967. *Visual Anthropology.* New York: Holt, Rinehart & Winston.

Curtiss, Deborah. 1987. *Introduction to Visual Literacy.* Englewood Cliffs, N.J.: Prentice-Hall.

DEKEN, JOSEPH. 1983. *Computer Images: State of the Art.* New York: Stewart, Tabori & Chang.

DONDIS, DONIS. 1973. *A Primer of Visual Literacy.* Cambridge, Mass.: M.I.T. Press.

EDWARDS, BETTY. 1979. *Drawing on the Right Side of the Brain.* Los Angeles: J. P. Tarcher.

EDWARDS, BETTY. 1986. *Drawing on the Artist Within.* New York: Simon & Schuster.

EISENSTEIN, SERGEI. 1942. *The Film Sense.* New York: Harvest/HBJ.

EISENSTEIN, SERGEI. 1949. *Film Form.* New York: Harvest/HBJ.

EISNER, ELLIOT W. 1972. *Educating Artistic Vision.* New York: Macmillan.

ESSLIN, MARTIN. 1982. *The Age of Television.* San Francisco: W. H. Freeman.

FELDMAN, EDMUND BURKE. 1973. *Varieties of Visual Experience.* New York: Abrams.

FRANSECKY, R. B., AND DEBES, JOHN L. 1972. *Visual Literacy.* Washington, D.C.: Association for Educational Communication.

GANDELMAN, CLAUDE. 1991. *Reading Pictures, Viewing Texts.* Bloomington, Ind.: Indiana University Press.

GATTEGNO, CALEB. 1969. *Towards a Visual Culture.* New York: Avon.

GOMBRICH, E. H. 1960. *Art and Illusion.* New York: Pantheon.

GOTSCHALK, D. W. 1947. *Art and the Social Order.* New York: Dover.

GOWANS, ALAN. 1971. *The Unchanging Arts: New Forms for the Traditional Functions of Art in Society.* Philadelphia: Lippincott.

GOWANS, ALAN. 1981. *Learning to See.* Bowling Green, Ohio: Bowling Green University Popular Press.

HALL, EDWARD T. 1969. *The Hidden Dimension.* New York: Anchor Books.

HANKS, KURT, ET AL. 1978. *Design Yourself.* Los Altos, Calif.: Kaufmann.

HANSON, JARICE. 1987. *Understanding Video.* Newbury Park, Calif.: Sage.

HOGG, JAMES, ED. 1970. *Psychology and the Visual Arts.* Baltimore: Penguin.

HUME, DAVID. 1949. *An Enquiry Concerning Human Understanding.* LaSalle, Ill.: The Open Court Publishing Company.

HUXLEY, ALDOUS. 1942. *The Art of Seeing.* New York: Harper.

JUNG, CARL, ED. 1964. *Man and His Symbols.* New York: Doubleday.

JUSSIM, ESTELLE. 1974. *Visual Communication and the Graphic Arts.* New York: Bowker.

KANIZSA, GAETANO. April 1976. "Subjective Contours." *Scientific American.* Reprinted in *Readings from the Scientific American: The Mind's Eye* (1986). Introductions by Jeremy M. Wolfe. New York: W. H. Freeman.

KANT, IMMANUEL. 1959 (1785). *Fundamental Principles of the Metaphysics of Morals.* Trans. Lewis W. Beck. New York: Liberal Arts Press.

KEPES, GYORGY. 1944. *Language of Vision.* Chicago: Paul Theobald.

KEPES, GYORGY. 1965. *Education of Vision.* New York: Braziller.

KRIS, ERNST. 1964. *Psychoanalytic Explorations in Art.* New York: Schocken.

LAKOFF, G., AND JOHNSON, M. 1980. *Metaphors We Live By.* Chicago: University of Chicago Press.

LIEBERMAN, J. BEN. 1968. *Types of Typefaces.* New York: Sterling.

LINDSTROM, MIRIAM. 1962. *Children's Art.* Berkeley: University of California Press.

McKIM, ROBERT H. 1980. *Thinking Visually.* Belmont, Calif.: Wadsworth.

McLUHAN, MARSHALL. 1965. *Understanding Media: The Extensions of Man.* New York: McGraw-Hill.

MEHRABIAN, ALBERT. 1971. *Silent Messages.* Belmont, Calif.: Wadsworth.

MESSARIS, PAUL. 1994. *Visual Literacy: Image, Mind & Reality.* Boulder, Colo.: Westview Press.

MOHOLY-NAGY, LASZLO. 1947. *Vision in Motion.* Chicago: Paul Theobald.

MONACO, JAMES. 1977. *How to Read a Film.* New York: Oxford University Press.

MORIARTY, SANDRA R. 1996. "Abduction: A Theory of Visual Interpretation." *Communication* (May).

NOLL, A. MICHAEL. 1967. "Computers and the Visual Arts." *Design and Planning #2.* New York: Hastings House.

NOLL, A. MICHAEL. 1982. Catalogue of SIGGRAPH art show.

NOVITZ, DAVID. 1977. *Pictures and Their Use in Communication*. The Hague: Martinus Nijhoff.

ORNSTEIN, ROBERT E. 1972. *The Psychology of Consciousness*. San Francisco: W. H. Freeman.

PAIVIO, ALLAN. 1979. *Imagery and Verbal Processes*. Hillsdale, N.J.: Lawrence Erlbaum.

PEIRCE, C. S. 1931–1958. *Collected Papers*. Cambridge, Mass.: Harvard University Press.

PREBLE, DUANE AND SARAH. 1985. *Artforms*. New York: Harper & Row.

PRYLUCK, CALVIN. 1976. *Sources of Meaning in Motion Pictures & Television*. New York: Arno Press.

REITBERGER, RHEINHOLD, AND FUCHS, WOLFGANG. 1972. *Comics: Anatomy of a Mass Medium*. Boston: Little, Brown.

SABIN, ROGER. 1993. *Adult Comics: An Introduction*. New York: Routledge.

SAUSSURE, FERDINAND DE. 1966. *Course in General Linguistics*. New York: McGraw-Hill.

SCHWARTZ, TONY. 1974. *The Responsive Chord*. New York: Doubleday.

SEBEOK, THOMAS A. 1979. *The Sign and Its Masters*. Austin: University of Texas Press.

SOLOMON, JACK. 1990. *The Signs of Our Time: The Secret Meanings of Everyday Life*. New York: Harper & Row.

SONTAG, SUSAN. 1966. *Against Interpretation*. New York: Farrar, Straus & Giroux.

SONTAG, SUSAN. 1973. *On Photography*. New York: Farrar, Straus & Giroux.

STERN, RAPHAEL AND ESTER. 1983. *Changing Concepts of Art*. New York: Haven.

TAYLOR, JOSHUA C. 1975. *To See Is to Think: Looking at American Art*. Washington, D.C.: Smithsonian Institution.

UDE-PESTEL, ANNELIESE. 1977. *Betty: History and Art of a Child in Therapy*. Palo Alto, Ca.: Science and Behavior Books.

WILEMAN, R. E. 1980. *Exercises in Visual Thinking*. New York: Hastings House.

WOLFE, JEREMY M. 1986. "Preface" and "Introductions" in *Readings from the Scientific American's The Mind's Eye*. 1986. Introductions by Jeremy Wolfe. New York: W. H. Freeman.

WORTH, SOL. 1981. *Studying Visual Communication*. Philadelphia: University of Pennsylvania Press.

YOUNGBLOOD, GENE. 1970. *Expanded Cinema*. New York: Dutton.

ZETTL, HERBERT. 1973. *Sight, Sound, Motion*. Belmont, Calif.: Wadsworth.

ILLUSTRATION CREDITS

All illustrations not otherwise credited have been provided by the author.

Introduction

0.3, 0.4, 0.5 Courtesy of Annaliese Ude-Pestel, author of Betty: History and Art of a Child in Therapy.

0.6 Courtesy of Apple Computer, Inc. and Chiat/Day Advertising.

0.7 Photo by Alice Shaw. Courtesy of Braunstein/Quay Gallery.

0.8 © Pixar. All Rights Reserved.

0.9 NASA

0.10 a,b Jason Berger

0.11 Courtesy of National Portrait Gallery, Smithsonian Institution, Washington, D.C.

0.12 Hirshhorn Museum and Sculpture Garden, Smithsonian Institution, Gift of the Joseph H. Hirshhorn Foundation, 1972.

0.13 Reproduced by permission of Varityper Corporation.

0.14 Courtesy of The Museum of Modern Art, New York, Film Stills Archive.

0.15 From Signs, Symbols & Ornaments by Rene Smeets. Copyright © 1975, 1982 by Van Nostrand Reinhold Company. Reprinted by permission; Reprinted with permission of Apple Computer Company.

Chapter 1

1.1 Ally & Gargano Advertising. Art Director, Ron Arnold. Copywriter, Tom Messner.

1.3 Foote, Cone & Belding Advertising. Reproduced courtesy of Levi Strauss & Co.

1.4 Illustration by Lorelle Raboni in "Eye Movements and Visual Perception" by David Norton and Lawrence Stark, Scientific American, June 1971, p. 37, bottom. Copyright © 1971 Scientific American, Inc. All Rights Reserved.

1.5 Hirshhorn Museum and Sculpture Garden, Smithsonian Institution, Museum Purchase with Funds Provided under the Smithsonian Institution Collections Acquisitions Program, 1981.

Chapter 2

2.8 Courtesy of Landor Associates and General Motors Corporation.

2.9 Courtesy of General Mills, Inc.

2.13 Reprinted with permission of Smith/Greenland, Inc.

2.16 Courtesy of The Museum of Modern Art, New York, Film Stills Archive.

2.17 Courtesy of National Gallery Publications Limited.

Chapter 3

3.8 Courtesy of Safeway Stores, Inc.

3.9 Courtesy of Cosmair, Inc.

3.10 Used by permission of Hal Riney & Partners, San Francisco, California.

3.15 Reprinted with permission of Smith/Greeland, Inc.

3.16 Samuel H. Kress Collection, Philbrook Museum of Art, Tulsa, Oklahoma.

3.17 With permission of The Absolut Company.

Chapter 4

4.1, 4.2, 4.10, 4.11, 4.12 Used by permission of the White House.

4.3 a,b, 4.5, 4.7 Courtesy of The Museum of Modern Art, New York, Film Stills Archive.

4.4 Reproduced by permission of Studies in Visual Communication, a journal devoted to visual anthropology.

4.6 Photo by Nicole Bengiveno. Used by permission of the San Francisco Ballet.

4.8, 4.9 Used by permission of the San Francisco Ballet.

4.13 © Ansel Adams. Reproduced courtesy of the National Archives.

4.14 a,b Photos by Richard Noble. © Time, Inc. Reprinted with permission.

4.15 Hirshhorn Museum and Sculpture Garden, Smithsonian Institution, Thomas M. Evans, Jerome L. Greene, Joseph H. Hirshhorn, and Sydney and Frances Lewis Purchase Fund, 1985.

Chapter 5

5.1, 5.2, 5.4, 5.6, 5.8, 5.9, 5.10 Courtesy of The Museum of Modern Art, New York, Film Stills Archive.

5.7 Used with permission of Gilbert Shelton.

Chapter 6

6.6 Reproduced with permission of Levi Strauss & Company and Foote, Cone & Belding.

6.7 Reproduced by permission of Apple Computer, Inc.

6.8 Used with permission of George Legrady.

6.9, 6.10 Reproduced by permission of Lynn Hershman.

Chapter 7

7.1a Reprinted by permission of Tribune Media Services; **7.1b** Used with permission of Gilbert Shelton.

7.2 Courtesy of The Museum of Modern Art, New York, Film Stills Archive.

7.5 Reproduced with permission of Care-Tech Laboratories.

7.8 Used with permission of George Legrady.

7.9 © The Main Line Company, Rockport, ME. Used with permission.

Chapter 8

8.1 Photograph by David Powers. Used with permission of the San Francisco Opera.

8.2, 8.4, 8.8 Reprinted with permission of U&lc, Internal Journal of Typographics.

8.3 From Rookledge's International Typefinder. Reproduced with kind permission of Sarema Press (Publishers) Limited of London, England.

8.5 American Committee for the Weizmann Institute of Science. Used with permission.

8.6 Used with permission of Hal Riney & Partners, San Francisco, California.

8.11 Reprinted by permission of The Wall Street Journal. © 1997 Dow Jones & Company, Inc. All Rights Reserved.

8.12 Used with permission of Detroit Free Press.

8.15 Used with permission of New Management.

8.16 Used by permission of The Gannett Center for Media Studies, Columbia University, New York.

Chapter 9

9.1 Courtesy of The Museum of Modern Art, New York, Film Stills Archive.

9.3 From P.M. Insel and W.T. Roth, Core Concepts in Health, Eighth Edition, Mayfield, 1997. Used with permission.

9.4 Used with permission Howard Rheingold.

9.6 Used with permission from Ulead Systems.

9.7 © Pixar.

9.8 Courtesy of Island Graphics Corporation. Reproduced with permission.

9.9 Photography by Marty Sohl. Courtesy of San Francisco Ballet.

9.10a Used with permission from A. Michael Noll; **9.10b** Used with permission from the Kröller-Müller Foundation.

NAMES INDEX

SUBJECT INDEX